GOD'S
POWER
TO
SAVE

GOD'S
POWER

One gospel for a complex world? | Edited by Chris Green

TO
SAVE

Oak Hill Annual School Of Theology

APOLLOS (an imprint of Inter-Varsity Press)
38 De Montfort Street, Leicester LE1 7GP, England
Website: www.ivpbooks.com
Email: ivp@ivp-editorial.co.uk

First published 2006

British Library Cataloguing in Publication Data
A catalogue record for this book is available from the British Library.

ISBN–13: 978–1–84474–134–2
ISBN–10: 1–84474–134–6

Set in Monotype Garamond 11/13pt
Typeset in Great Britain by Servis Filmsetting Ltd, Manchester
Printed and bound in Great Britain by Creative Print & Design (Wales),
Ebbw Vale

CONTENTS

CONTRIBUTORS

Simon Gathercole is Senior Lecturer in New Testament in the Department of Divinity and Religious Studies, University of Aberdeen.

Chris Green is Vice-Principal and Lecturer in Mission, Ministry Strategy and Perspectives and Homiletics, Oak Hill College.

Michael Ovey is Lecturer in Doctrine, Apologetics and Philosophy, Oak Hill College.

David Peterson is Principal and Lecturer in New Testament Studies, Oak Hill College.

James Robson is Lecturer in Old Testament Studies, Oak Hill College.

Paul Woodbridge is Lecturer in New Testament Studies, Oak Hill College.

ABBREVIATIONS

BTB	*Biblical Theology Bulletin*
ESV	English Standard Version
ExpT	*Expository Times*
Hist. eccl.	*Historia ecclesiastica*
JBL	*Journal of Biblical Literature*
JETS	*Journal of the Evangelical Theological Society*
JSNT	*Journal for the Study of the New Testament*
JSNTSup	Journal for the Study of the New Testament: Supplement
JTS	*Journal of Theological Studies*
NAC	New American Commentary
NIGTC	New International Greek Testament Commentary
NICNT	New International Commentary on the New Testament
NIVAC	NIV Application Commentary
NRSV	New Revised Standard Version
NT	New Testament
NTS	*New Testament Studies*
RTR	*Reformed Theological Review*
SBET	*Scottish Bulletin of Evangelical Theology*
SBT	Studies in Biblical Theology
TynBul	*Tyndale Bulletin*
VTSup	Vetus Testamentum Supplements
WBC	Word Biblical Commentary
WUNT	Wissenschaftliche Untersuchungen zum Neuen Testament

INTRODUCTION

Chris Green

The *Oak Hill School of Theology* is an annual event in our calendar, which takes several years to plan and publish. The initial selection of the theme, and the choice of speakers for the day, is done two years ahead of time, and the contributors then begin to read, think, interact and pray around their given areas. Frequent conversations and shared reading give a cohesion and collaborative feel to the venture, and then each speaker in turn delivers an early version of the paper to the rest of the faculty. Again, interchange takes place, and the papers are reworked until the School itself. After that, the constraints of a 50-minute talk are lifted, and each writer is freed to expand the paper into a chapter for this book.

It sounds like the work of an enclosed community, although it's actually more like the work of a group of close Christian friends. But what happens each time is that the subject we have chosen gains a resonance and power, until its relevance to the contemporary church becomes inescapable.

So it was with the themes of 'one gospel, many gospels' and 'speaking truth in a pluralistic and tolerant world'. Who would have guessed that one of the contributors would be dividing his time between writing his chapter and drafting amendments for the House of Lords on the issue of freedom of religious speech? The issues of whether Christian truth is not only truth but, as Francis Schaeffer used to put it, *true* truth, and whether that gives the liberty to declare that other views are therefore non-truth is at the forefront of contemporary debate.

In the more rarefied atmosphere of New Testament studies, the issue is less starkly expressed, but still forcefully present. Generations of young students have left their theological studies persuaded that the Synoptic Gospels and John, or the Synoptic Gospels and Paul, or indeed Paul and Jesus, have such mutually exclusive views that they cannot be made to sit together with intellectual honesty. Talk of diversity in the New Testament could well be seen to be a cover for talk of divergence.

This chimes with the students' wider experience of contemporary Britain, where tolerance of divergence is such an accepted cultural norm that it seems crude to expect agreement, compliance or even submission in intellectual debate. What are such students to do when, speaking at an evangelistic event, they are confronted by an intelligent atheist who claims (with scholarly support) that Paul invented Christianity, or a gentle pluralist who claims that Jesus' message was tolerance and Christians show a marked lack of it, or a forceful Muslim who claims that the New Testament is manifestly full of contradictions and that it is the perfect Qur'an which is true, or a gay rights activist who claims that today we must be tolerant of everything except intolerance, or with an earnest Student Union politician who claims that the only sustainable *modus vivendi* is for everyone to give up their claims to exclusivity, or . . .? How are the young evangelists to respond? And what are they to do with a nagging feeling that they are out on an indefensible limb?

Dr Michael Ovey opens the book with a consideration of what it means for contemporary Britain to claim to be a pluralist culture. Michael teaches Doctrine at Oak Hill, and his clarity with the often complex subject he deals with in his chapter is extremely helpful. Moreover, before he was ordained, Michael was a barrister, and one who regularly drafted legislation that came before the Houses of Parliament. This gives his chapter two unique elements.

First, Michael is acutely aware of, and sensitive to, the political consequences of trends in society and public life, and of the echoing trends in theology. His opening scenarios not only cover a hilariously inept piece of theological education, but the selection (and subsequent deselection) of an EU commissioner, and the arrest of an elderly man in a British seaside town. There is no hiding from public life in the kind of orthodoxy Michael models here, because he shows clearly how theology and politics converse and collide.

Second, his training as a barrister explains the forensic skill with which he dissects (I am tempted to say, vivisects) an argument and lays open its founding presuppositions and inevitable consequences. Michael is persuaded that the current praise being heaped upon tolerance springs from a deep rebellion against God, and to demonstrate that he digs far down into Western culture's foundations. Not many readers will be familiar with the writings of the Florentine Niccolò Machiavelli, nor with the Oxford political philosopher Isaiah Berlin, but as Michael lays the argument out there is no doubt we are being shown the route by which many of our contemporaries can hold two incompatible thoughts, and for it not to worry them. This is unfamiliar territory in which to find an evangelical, but if the tides in our society are as this chapter describes, then we shall need to become much more familiar with these ideas if we are to fight for our fundamental intellectual freedoms.

One version of the idea of holding two incompatible thoughts simultaneously has been found in New Testament Studies, and much of the remainder of the book is given over to a critique of the idea that the New Testament contains a number of incompatible gospels. It is such a simple thought, but it has had such devastating impact on Biblical Studies that the writers considered it deserving of careful examination.

Dr Paul Woodbridge begins with an examination of the Fourth Gospel. Paul has been a lecturer in New Testament at Oak Hill for some considerable time, for much of which he has taught on John's Gospel. His first chapter explores the difference in terminology between John and the Synoptics, and the content which the former expresses in the phrase 'eternal life' and the latter in 'kingdom of God'. Superficially they are different, but Paul is convinced they are conveying the same truths. His careful step-by-step approach, working through the reasons for the lack of references to the 'kingdom' in John, and the way the Synoptics use 'eternal life', ends with arguing for considerable consistent overlap between the two terms in both bodies of literature. His conclusions are modest, and his method persuasive.

In his second chapter, Paul narrows the focus down to the Fourth Gospel, and to the term 'eternal life'. Once again we have careful exegesis, and precisely nuanced conclusions along the way. But the final triumphant conclusion, which is reached by way of understanding the mission and glorification of Jesus, casts new light on the meaning of the term. It is, Paul argues, eternal life *in the kingdom*. The two terms are, to use his word, 'co-referential'.

So a major brick has been removed from the wall between John and the Synoptics. As Paul moves through contemporary scholarship it becomes clear this is no isolated phenomenon, nor is he alone in thinking along these lines. The polarization between John and the Synoptics, which conceded – perhaps even demanded – that there were irreconcilable differences, and which therefore enthroned what Michael Ovey calls 'incommensurable pluralism', seems to be coming to an end, and a more balanced and synthesizing approach emerges.

My chapter, which follows, goes into waters that are less well-charted and where the storms are only beginning. The book of Acts has been re-emerging in New Testament studies after a period of neglect, and is beginning to attract some attention; not all of it helpful. Why, for instance, does Luke hardly mention the kingdom of God, or Jesus' death? An argument similar to the one explaining the difference between the Synoptics and John has emerged, in which there are different, and fundamentally irreconcilable, gospels within the work of even one writer. I attempt to show that this is to misread Acts: the references to the kingdom are few, but they occur at such signally important points in the narrative that their relative scarcity becomes a non-issue. Moreover, I argue that if one moves from looking at 'kingdom' to the rule and honorifics of the 'King', a much deeper theology of the cross and resurrection emerges. Having come the back way into the Synoptic authors, I then turn to Mark. To describe Mark's theology of the

kingdom briefly is not possible, but I try to give some innovative
ways through, particularly by starting with the last reference to the
kingdom, which I argue is a resurrection reference, and the last
reference to the King, which is above Jesus on the cross. Glancing
through the one passage in Matthew/Luke that might mean the
kingdom is inaugurated in some way other than the cross, I then
look at the kingdom of God in the Old Testament, and why the
concept is there even though the phrase is absent.

Dr Simon Gathercole continues our reconstruction with a
wide-ranging survey of the gospel in the writings of Paul. Simon is
the one contributor who is not on the Oak Hill Faculty; instead, he
teaches New Testament at the University of Aberdeen, and has
published several widely acclaimed books and articles on Pauline
theology. At issue in his chapter is the charge that Paul invented a
completely new gospel, which is radically different from the
message of Jesus. It is the claim, still widely heard, that Paul
invented Christianity from the much simpler, and less doctrinal,
message of Jesus. Once again, Simon does careful work and slowly
builds his case: he shows what the Pauline message is, and argues
that Jesus the Messiah's sin-bearing death and his resurrection
bring atonement and a new creation. Having established that, he
then examines the evidence from the Gospels to argue that this is
the perspective that they, too, share. He argues this not by trying to
twist the few references to 'kingdom' in Paul to match the gospel
references, nor by trying to argue that 'righteousness of God' and
'the kingdom of God' are different words for the same concept.
Rather, he argues that the Synoptics and Paul share a deep similarity in their theology, and Jesus' Messianic identity, his atoning and
justifying death and his inauguration of a new dominion by his
resurrection form the irreplaceable core.

Professor David Peterson's chapter is an attempt to synthesize
what has gone before, and to map out a new paradigm for unifying
the New Testament. David is a respected scholar and author, and
his mature reflections of a lifetime of academic study of the New
Testament show the benefit of the long view. As a student he was
deeply impressed by C. H. Dodd, and his attempt to provide a
simple, synthesized New Testament message: the kerygma. David
was also deeply challenged by the attempt of J. D. G. Dunn to show

that Dodd had oversimplified the New Testament to a dangerous degree, and that the reality was more complex, more diverse and more irreconcilable than Dodd allowed. David's chapter revisits the Dodd versus Dunn debate, and using both his material and the arguments in the preceding chapters demonstrates that although the reality is more complex than Dodd allowed, it is not *that* much more complex, and that Dunn's case, when subjected to careful scrutiny, does not hold. For some reason, perhaps for the reasons that Michael Ovey's chapter outlines, Dunn's thesis won wide and substantial support from the late 1970s when it was first published, and it is still a standard text in undergraduate studies. If David Peterson is right, however, as he carefully works through the evidence from Paul, Acts, John and the Synoptics, there is inescapable evidence for the case for unity of message across the New Testament, and the position Dunn adopts needs to be avoided.

This issue is close to the academic heart of this book, but it would be wrong to think that any of the authors see this as merely an 'academic' (in the sense of 'interesting but irrelevant') issue. As the chapters repeatedly show, the matter to hand is whether God has *truly* made himself known, or is a bundle of high-sounding contradictions; whether the New Testament shares God's consistency, or his (its/their?) pluralities and rivalries; whether tolerance of irreconcilable truth claims is a virtue or a lie; whether there is one gospel that is true for all people, everywhere, or if there is a range of presentable options among which one may choose; whether the assertion that the gospel *is the power of God for salvation to everyone who believes* (Rom. 1:16) is true or not.

The passion in those questions explains the final chapter. None of the papers in the volume was presented at the School of Theology in the form in which it now appears, and David Peterson's was not given at all on the day. But we decided that the final emphasis in the book must not lie with intellectual argument, no matter how persuasively made, but with a passionate preaching of God's Word. Dr James Robson teaches Old Testament at Oak Hill, and he summarized in one sermon – which was not preached with a view to publication, but only to move his hearers – what it means to know, love and serve the one, true, living, speaking God, to whom be the glory.

Note

The practice followed in this volume is to abbreviate all the biblio-
graphical information in footnotes, so making any argument stand
out. A reference, for example, to Schaeffer 1970:27 should take the
reader to the bibliography at the back, to find listed Schaeffer, F.
(1970), *The God Who Is There* (London: Hodder & Stoughton), and
thence to page 27. Lengthy articles in dictionaries are referred to
by the author and title of the article, and then to the dictionary
itself.

1. CAN WE SPEAK OF 'THE' GOSPEL IN A POSTMODERN WORLD? PLURALISM, POLYTHEISM AND THE GOSPEL OF THE ONE, TRUE GOD

Michael Ovey

. . . the virtues do more terrible damage[1]

Introduction

We sometimes hear the charge that modern Britain, like other modern Western countries, is a somewhat immoral place. Old-style Marxists used to speak of the decadent capitalist West. Current Middle Eastern mullahs speak of its satanic character. Classic evangelicals likewise have decried how unethical many aspects of our national life have become, on areas ranging from embryo experimentation, to sexual faithfulness, to financial probity. It seems obvious to us. So it is perhaps worth remembering how modern Britain outside the churches can think of itself very much as a moral country, with strong ethical standards, not least because of its self-image as increasingly a model of pluralistic

---

1. Chesterton 1909:51.

virtue, a country in which all kinds of diversity thrive. Possessing
such pluralistic virtue can seem to be a, perhaps the, ground of
moral self-congratulation, and acquiring greater degrees of pluralistic virtue an appropriate national aspiration.

Some snapshots

However, let us now look at some snapshots on how virtuously
pluralist Britain can work. First of all, and central to the theme of
this book, is the 'gospel on a plate'. This requires some explanation.
There was a training course in one of our major denominations
that made extensive use of paper plates. This was not for practice
in how to run a vicarage tea party with copious thin-sliced cucum-
ber sandwiches; the point rather was that participants would all sit
in a circle and pass the paper plate round to each other. Each
person would be asked to write on the plate what the gospel was for
them, and pass it on for the next person to do the same. The plate
would then be taken by the person running the exercise, who would
read out the inscriptions and say, 'This is the gospel for us.' Of
course, by the time the plate had circulated round a relatively large
and diverse group, the various accounts of the gospel were not just
differently nuanced but actually downright contradictory. But all
were allowed to stand side by side.

Our second snapshot stays within the major denominations.
One theological college instituted the practice on day one for its
new students of taking them through Mark's account of the
feeding of the five thousand. So far, so good. However, each
student was asked what the incident means. Characteristically, one
would say it was a miracle demonstrating Jesus is the Son of God.
Another would refer it to the Lord's Supper. Another would say it
was not miraculous but was an acted parable on the redistribution
of wealth. And so on. No interpretation was criticized by the
tutor, none preferred above others: all were allowed to stand. All
the meanings, at any rate those currently in play, the conduct
implies, were valid.

Next, imagine the scene at a British seaside town. An elderly
man was surrounded, being harassed and jostled by a crowd of

much younger and fitter men. Fortunately, the police were shortly on the scene and made an arrest – of the elderly man. The elderly man had a placard saying that homosexuality was sinful and incurred God's wrath. So, naturally, the group of homosexuals and their sympathizers felt obliged to vent their disgust by physical assault. Mercifully, or not, the elderly victim of the assault, Harry Hammond, was successfully prosecuted under Britain's law and order legislation. If you like, the homosexuals' right to be outraged could not be compared or evaluated against other considerations.

Our last snapshot remains with so-called fundamental freedoms, but features the EU and the strange case of Rocco Buttiglione, a distinguished Roman Catholic intellectual. He was, we may remember, the man who considered practising homosexuality sinful but also that it should not be criminalized, a conventional enough distinction between moral evaluation and what should be illegal. We may also recall that various European lobby groups successfully opposed his installation as an EU commissioner. The grounds of opposition repay attention. It was not because of any action of his in public office nor any proposal of his concerning public policy, but rather because of his personal opinions and religious beliefs. Remarkably, perhaps, little mention was made, certainly in the media in this country, about European commitment to freedom of belief or, come to that, to UN commitments against religious discrimination. Rather, in the name of plural Europe, an entire raft of people with particular beliefs, including, it may well be, many evangelicals in the United Kingdom, had in principle been excluded from public office at that level of the EU, because of their personal beliefs, even when those beliefs did not result in any different conduct of public office. One naturally wonders what other jobs such lobby groups may deem one unfit to fill.

What's at stake? The question of plurality

Each of these snapshots features in some sense the question of plurality, plural accounts of the gospel, plural interpretations of the Bible, plural beliefs about sexuality, often with the sense

'there's no wrong answer' – with the proviso, of course, that we
must all accept there is no wrong answer. What would be wrong
would be the suggestion that some answers are wrong. These are
attitudes many Christians no doubt meet from time to time in our
evangelistic or apologetic ministries.

It is perhaps, though, worth briefly recalling how that proposition 'There's no wrong answer' comes to be asserted. We
sometimes hear a false dichotomy that goes like this:

- *Either* we have exhaustive, 'monolithic' understandings. (We
  might paraphrase these understandings as asserting, 'This is all
  there is to it' or 'I've got it completely taped.')
- *Or* unrestrictedly plural understandings. (We might paraphrase
  this as asserting, 'It could mean this, could mean that, but I have
  no ultimate vantage point from which to rule any idea in or
  out.')

The argument then runs that if we cannot claim *exhaustive* understanding (the first part of the dichotomy), we can be left only with
the alternative 'there's no wrong answer'. That is, after all, the only
remaining possibility on this argument.

It has frequently been pointed out over the last forty years (at
least) that this is a false dilemma.[2] Why? The reality is far less crude
than this dilemma allows. Evangelicals (like others) do accept
levels of meaning, for example over Old Testament prefigurings
of Christ and the fact that God brings forth fresh light from his
Word. One reason why evangelicals delight to preach and study
the same passages many times is precisely because we think God
does bring us to further and deeper understandings of his infallible and inerrant Word. However, the point is this: God does not
bring forth *inconsistent* light. He does not one minute bring forth
the truth that Jesus is fully man and fully God and then at a later
stage bring forth the truth that Jesus is not. We believe in a God
who is eternally truthful and that implies a consistency to what he
says.

---

2. Notably see Schaeffer 1968.

We should not here confuse 'exhaustive' with 'excluding'. We may well say we do not have an *exhaustive* understanding of the statement 'God is holy,' for instance, but we would say even our non-exhaustive understanding *excludes* certain things, like, obviously, 'God is not holy.' For when we make any positive predication about God and say that God is something or some quality (such as 'God is just'), then that positive predication carries an excluding sense, for it necessarily implies that God is not the contradiction of that quality (in our example 'God is just' rules out 'God is not just'). If we deny this and say that 'God is just' does not exclude 'God is not just', then naturally people would ask us whether the first statement 'God is just' actually meant anything.[3]

Plurality with or without coherence
This takes us to a truer dichotomy within which to consider pluralism. The dichotomy is between two kinds of plurality. On the one hand, there is a plurality which envisages that, although there is plurality and diversity of authentic values and virtues that bind humans, there is still coherence between the various elements. On the other hand, there is a plurality of authentic values and virtues that bind humans where there is no coherence between all of the elements. We could illustrate this diagrammatically thus:

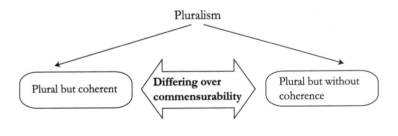

3. Similarly, Reformed theology of John Owen's period (1616–83) distinguished archetypal from ectypal theological knowledge: archetypal knowledge is the self-knowledge God has of himself and is complete and infallible. Ectypal knowledge, the kind humans have, is not complete but is nevertheless genuine in so far as it rests on God's self-knowledge and arises from his revelation.

A key notion lying between these two different ways of seeing plurality is commensurability. This somewhat cumbersome word is chosen because one particular kind of pluralism uses this notion. Commensurability, of course, relates to the idea that two things can be properly measured against each other, so that there is some legitimate standard of comparison. Thus in arithmetic, two fractions (say three-quarters and two-thirds) can be properly measured against each other when put in terms of a common denominator (in the example, they would be nine-twelfths and eight-twelfths). With a common denominator we can work out which is greater, how they can be added and so on.

To return to our different kinds of pluralism, in the 'plural but coherent' category, one can ultimately measure one element against another. They can be related in some way. We might say that a common denominator exists and therefore they are commensurable. In the plural but without coherence category, one cannot measure or compare one element against another. We can illustrate this with a commonplace example. We use the maxim 'You can't compare apples and oranges.' The maxim reminds us that some things are simply different and comparisons are inappropriate. They taste different and most aptly fulfil different types of physical appetite, hunger and thirst. On that basis, how can one compare? An apple is not meant to taste like an orange, and we choose first one, now the other, depending on what appetite we wish to satisfy or what sensation we wish to enjoy. Such thinking emphasizes plurality without coherence.

Yet we can run the apples and oranges question another way. In another sense, we do sometimes compare apples and oranges. One might see apples at £5 an apple and compare it unfavourably to oranges at 30p each. Here there is a medium through which we can compare: money is the common denominator. It emphasizes plurality with coherence.

Thus on, say, Old Testament prefigurings of Christ, we may well admit plurality of meaning, but contend that the meanings are related and coherent – they are not incommensurable. The Passover lambs of Exodus and the Passover Lamb who is the Lord Jesus bear related meanings. This is not to claim they are at all points the same, nor that we necessarily exhaustively understand each. Yet, if we interpret the Exodus lambs and the New Testament Passover Lamb in contradictory ways, then we would in principle be committed to a plurality without coherence. We would also have enormous difficulty in specifying how the Exodus lambs actually do prefigure Christ.

Let us apply this framework of plurality with and without commensurability to the snapshots we first looked at. In those examples there are strong patterns of incommensurability. In the first example, of many differing accounts of the gospel written on the plate, the acceptance of high degrees of inconsistency between the different elements suggests plurality without coherence or commensurability: different accounts of the gospel seem incommensurable. Similarly, with the various interpretations of the feeding of the five thousand. Concerning Harry Hammond and Rocco Buttiglione, the value of their freedom of expression or freedom of religion does not seem to be compared, at least in the public mind, with the alternative rights, the right not to be offended and the right to have public figures personally approve of one's sexual choices. In the Buttiglione case there appeared to be no weighing of competing rights. Incommensurability seems indicated in these cases by the way that the right not to be offended and the right to have public figures personally approve of one's sexual choices apparently function unchecked, and are, so to speak, 'trump cards'.

The aim in what follows is not to provide a global explanation of 'pluralism'. There are arguments for different kinds of pluralism, and lack of space precludes my dealing with all of them. Instead, this chapter aims to draw out one theme in pluralist thinking – the question of incommensurability. There is more to contemporary pluralism, and there may be better pluralisms, than this, but incommensurability is a highly significant theme. Let me explain why.

Why does incommensurable pluralism matter?

Obviously, one wonders why incommensurable pluralism should matter to Christians. Two areas immediately spring to mind: first, that of our biblical duties, and second, that of our place in the public square.

Biblical duties

In terms of our biblical duties, Titus 1:9 and Acts 20 (where Paul addresses the Ephesian elders at Miletus) lay some clear and significant duties on all ministers. Titus 1:9 tells us to encourage the flock by sound teaching and to refute those who oppose it. It is worth noting that Paul's word is 'refute' or 'rebuke' (*elenchein*). 'Refute' is a strong term,[4] which implies specifying where and why that false teaching is wrong.[5] In a similar vein, Acts 20:28–31 warns us to protect the flock; notably, against those even arising from within the presbyterate who will bring forth false teaching.

Yet if claims to truth are incommensurable, we cannot say 'this biblical truth precludes that view'. Evangelistically we could not say, as Paul and Barnabas did in Acts 14:15, that the Lystrans should turn from these worthless things. For, if claims to truth are incommensurable, one could not simply call the Lystran idols 'worthless things'. Such judgments could be made only from within our own system, and do not have a universal binding nature. One therefore should not insist the Lystrans are obliged to 'turn' from these 'worthless things'. Paul and Barnabas unmistakeably think the Lystrans are doing wrong as they seek to offer sacrifice.[6] If claims to truth really are incommensurable, the gospel loses its character of proclamation, and evangelism is inhibited. Similarly, within a local church or denomination for the same reasons, we cannot effectively pastor our flocks against false teaching. Similar

---

4. See Mounce 2000:392.

5. Note the use of *elenchein* in forensic and logical discourse with respect to a demonstrated argument; e.g. Aristotle in *Sophistical Refutations* is dealing with invalid *arguments*, and defines 'refutation' in terms of argument thus: 'For to refute is to contradict one and the same attribute – not merely the name, but the reality – and a name that is not merely synonymous but the same name – and to confute it from the propositions granted, necessarily, without including in the reckoning the original point to be proved, in the same respect and relation and manner and time in which it was asserted' (*Sophistical Refutations* 1.5).

6. Compare Acts 17:30, where Paul envisages a general moral duty on pagans to repent.

considerations arise in applying Galatians 1:8. There Paul enjoins an anathema on those who preach another gospel (literally, 'alongside' [*para*], with the sense of something different).[7] For this to have meaning one must be able to see that something is not the same gospel as the one Paul taught. This requires some comparison of concepts.

This means that real care must be exercised over the claim to find 'different proclamations' within the biblical material. Recent years have seen claims not merely to provide different presentations of essentially the same gospel (as in the choice between using presentations of, say, *Two Ways to Live* rather than *Christianity Explored*), but also the idea that the New Testament material contains diverse gospels with different orientations; for example, in the idea that the gospel of Jesus is not the same as the gospel of Paul. There is a point where plurality becomes incoherent and comprises contradictory accounts.

The issue, though, is not whether the gospel must be taught and proclaimed in essentially the same words on all occasions. Misgivings about 'different gospels' are not necessarily insisting on that. For there are differences between Paul's proclamation in the synagogues at Berea and Thessalonica (Acts 17:2ff and 17:10ff), on the one hand, and his proclamation at the Areopagus, on the other (Acts 17:22–34). In the first case, he reasons about the fulfilment of the Old Testament Scriptures, and, in the second, he utilizes ideas from creation theology to convict the Athenians' idolatry. This framework admits plurality and diversity, but a coherent plurality.

The issue is, though, whether different proclamations, different kerygmata, are in a framework which entails that they are not commensurable. In such a case the framework is one of pluralism without coherence, and this generates enormous difficulty in giving due weight to the warnings of Galatians 1:9. As it happens, in the case of Paul's various proclamations in Acts 17, his work in the synagogues and on the Areopagus does represent a coherent diversity, because, of course, the same Old Testament that provides the

---

7. Porter 1994:167 stresses the idea of replacement. Wallace 1996:378 notes the sense of opposition that *para* can carry.

framework of promise and fulfilment in Jesus also provides the creation theology he uses on the Areopagus. The God who gave the promises to Israel is also the creator of heaven and earth.

More generally, outside the sphere of presbyteral responsibility, believers have a duty to give an account for the hope they have (1 Pet. 3:15) – this becomes far harder when common ground between believer and non-believer disappears, as incommensurable pluralism suggests. We shall return to the point that incommensurable pluralism destroys common ground.

Public square
Some developments of incommensurable pluralism can mean we lose the civic liberty to proclaim the gospel. This is an important claim and a surprising one, perhaps, for, as we shall see shortly, one of the claims often made for incommensurable pluralism is just that it preserves liberty. In that sense the case of Harry Hammond is indicative. And, of course, it is the nature of the gospel to cause offence. Paul himself notes that apostles bringing the gospel can be the smell of death to some (2 Cor. 2:16).

Given, then, that incommensurable pluralism is a matter of Christian concern, we must examine how this idea is generated and what supports it.

Incommensurable truths and values: the idea of Isaiah Berlin

Outline of Isaiah Berlin's idea
First, we must go to the highly influential Oxford historian of ideas, Isaiah Berlin (1909–97).[8] In his essay 'The Pursuit of the Ideal' Berlin outlines the germination and development of what some would see as his central idea, the incommensurability of

---

8. Isaiah Berlin taught for many years at Oxford, notably in the fields of political theory, and was the first President of Wolfson College. He had earlier held the Chichele chair of social and political theory from 1957 to 1967.

values.[9] Berlin suggests he arrived at this principle via consideration of, notably, Niccolò Machiavelli (1469–1527),[10] Giambattista Vico (1668–1744)[11] and Johann Gottfried von Herder (1744–1803),[12] all of whom undermined the idea of unique, single answers to human problems.[13] This idea of incommensurability of values forms the linchpin of a particularly famous and important essay of his called 'Two Concepts of Liberty'.[14]

Now, in discussing incommensurable values, Berlin is not just making a point about interpretation, the idea that we see different things in a text, whatever that text may be, whether *Beowulf*, the Bible or *Black Beauty*. Rather, Berlin's point is that there are genuine values, and they are genuinely disparate and compete with each other. As it happens, Berlin is not the originator of this idea. We can trace it much earlier, as he himself points out, but he is a highly influential and clear advocate. It is just his conspicuous ability that suggests we should spend time considering him.[15]

---

9. See Berlin 1998a.

10. Machiavelli, a Florentine public servant and man of letters, is best known, of course, for his short work on maintaining autocratic power, *The Prince*. His own preferred form of government, republicanism, is developed in *The Discourses*. His analysis has strong common features between the two works, although differently applied.

11. Vico was professor of Rhetoric at the University of Naples. He is best known for *The New Science*, which Berlin considered illuminated the way human creation is located and limited in particular historical environments.

12. Herder contributed notably to reflection on the relation between thought and language, and was a significant part of German reaction to the Enlightenment.

13. Berlin 1998a:6–9.

14. Berlin also calls this idea 'objective pluralism': here the description 'incommensurable pluralism' is preferred, because incommensurability is an idea Berlin frequently employs and 'objective' is dangerously ambiguous in this context.

15. Berlin's work on the history of ideas and his contributions to the analysis and influence of German Romanticism are of enduring value.

Berlin speaks of 'the fact that human goals are many, not all of them commensurable, and in perpetual rivalry with one another'.[16] Similarly, G. K. Chesterton had much earlier observed:

> The modern world is full of the old Christian virtues gone mad. The virtues have gone mad because they have been isolated from each other and are wandering alone. Thus some scientists care for truth; and their truth is pitiless. Thus some humanitarians care only for pity and their pity (I am sorry to say) is often untruthful.[17]

In support of his thesis, Berlin relied particularly on two points: first, that the idea of commensurable human goals was incoherent; and, second, that the idea of a single harmonious system of values and goals was dangerous.[18]

However, this argument is not simply saying, 'There are several genuine goods and we want to get a good balance between them: we must trade off between them to get the right answer.' On that view one can get better trade-offs or worse trade-offs, and one has a way of comparing trade-offs. In other words, there is a measure of commensurability, in the same way that we might compare twenty apples bought for £5 to forty oranges bought for £5. The Berlin point goes further. It is rather this: 'We have lots of goals, and since there is no real basis of comparison between them, trade-offs are arbitrary.'

The result is a proposition that goes like this: *humans have values, but they are set at war with each other.*

Comments on Berlin's idea

This proposition requires some comments. First, it is not always

---

16. Berlin 1998b:241.

17. Chesterton 1909:51.

18. Stated within short compass, and with Berlin's usual elegance, in Berlin 1998a:11, 12. As regards the incoherence point, see also Berlin 1997. Berlin 1998b:241 derives much of its power from the argument about danger.

clear whether Berlin thinks that all values or only some of them are at war in this way.[19] Thus one might think that some values, such as truthfulness, faithfulness and righteousness are closely related, such that a denial of one would involve denial of the others. Yet clearly, even if some values could be grouped into families in this kind of way, Berlin's arguments about incommensurability might still apply between families of values.

Second, in Berlin's view there is *inevitable* war between different values. He writes, 'These collisions of values are of the essence of what they are and what we are.'[20] The example often cited in support by Berlin and others agreeing with him is the conflict between liberty and equality. The perfect liberty of all may interfere with the equality of all. There is no way perfect liberty and perfect equality can coexist in the same society. It is for this reason that he thinks the idea of harmony among human values is simply incoherent.

However, there is some ambiguity and vagueness in the proposal that *humans have values, but they are set at war with each other.* To begin with, the statement that humans 'have values' is ambiguous. On the one hand, this might mean that humans think and act in terms of values, but we must always be agnostic about the real status of these values as to whether they are ultimately purely human constructions or not. On the other hand, this might mean that humans think and act in terms of values, some of which at least are not simply human constructions.

At this point, Berlin's own citation of Vico is highly illuminating. Amongst other things, Berlin reads Vico as suggesting that humans create and work in the context of particular cultures, so that what is possible in one culture is not so in another. The human framework that made possible the creation of the *Iliad* or the *Odyssey* is simply not there in other times and places.[21] It is, it seems, this incommensurability of cultures that Berlin reads in

---

19. Thus Berlin 1998a:7 merely speaks of 'Not all' the supreme values being consistent.

20. Berlin 1998a:11.

21. See e.g. Berlin 1998a:7–8; cf. Berlin 1997:123–124.

Vico, and from this he envisages an incommensurability of values. 'Values' here seems to refer primarily to values as human constructions, albeit possibly unintentional ones.

If this reading of Berlin is right, then there would be clear dangers in adopting him for Christian theologians committed to the idea that values are not simply human constructions but reflect the mind and will of God.

One also wonders quite how Berlin can be so sure that the claims of those who do believe in values revealed by God are wrong – the criticisms about incoherence seem to imply this very strongly. He clearly does think values are not revealed by God, yet such global adjudications of wrongness are precisely the things that his theory of incommensurable pluralism rules out in other cases. It is difficult not to sense some incoherence here.

Further, the part of the proposition that suggests values are 'at war with each other' also needs some further probing. If there are such things as divinely revealed values and there are such things as values that are purely human constructions, then the conflict can be one between what God wills and what humans will. Even the possibility of such conflict does not seem to be contemplated by Berlin's scheme. On this view, his account of the kinds of conflicts that occur between values is too simplistic. Instead of the simple idea that values are at war, we should recognize two distinct wars of values. There may well be war between two sets of values that are both purely human constructions. Christians might well expect just this, given our finitude and our fallenness. But there may well be (and Christians would insist there are) conflicts between values willed by God and values willed by finite and fallen men and women. However, Berlin's argument in effect means that we could not call 'sin' the willing by humans of values that contradict God's. Orthodox Christians would add that this is both an attraction and a danger in the idea of incommensurable pluralism.

We should add finally under this question of vagueness and ambiguity, the question of what Berlin means by a 'value'. Berlin suggests that liberty and equality inevitably conflict. So they do – on his definitions. Yet it is not absurd to envisage different definitions that avoid conflict; for example, that 'real' liberty does not extend to harming others, and that such harm is an abuse of liberty and a distortion of it. Nor is it absurd to envisage definitions of liberty and equality which are in some way given a common denominator and made commensurable; for example, by rooting both in ideas of what is due to a human individual.[22] Berlin (understandably, given his commitment to particular forms of plural civic life) has rather different ideas of liberty and equality in mind. It is not obvious, though, why his definitions should be accepted, and if we do not accept his definitions, then his insistence on the *inevitability* of conflict of values is far weaker.

Third, Berlin insists that the field of possible human values is not unending: 'Ends, moral principles, are many. But not infinitely many: they must be within the human horizon. If they are not, then they are outside the human sphere.'[23]

The result of this is that for Berlin, and the more sophisticated derivatives of his theory, we cannot accept each and every value as privileged by incommensurable pluralism as legitimate goals of human endeavour. Within the sphere of 'the human horizon', particular goals are to be allowed to flourish, because the principle of incommensurable pluralism protects them from falsification. Outside that sphere, goals are not necessarily to be so allowed.

When applying this principle, Berlin uses the example of those who worship wood. Some reasons for worshipping wood he finds himself able to understand, if not accept. One reason, though, he does not understand, and he says of those who hold it: 'They are not human for me. I cannot even call their values subjective if I cannot conceive what it would be like to pursue such a life.'[24]

These are disturbing words. The litmus test, it seems, for accepting a particular idea within the scope of allowable incom-

---

22. A not unusual basis for justice, comparable to the Aristotelian idea of rendering to each what he deserves.

23. 1998a:10.

24. 1998a:10.

mensurable pluralism is whether or not an onlooker finds this idea conceivable and one with which he can sympathize. Of course, it may be difficult to conceive following a set of ideas because of some fault in the ideas: they are so repugnant, perhaps. One may find it is inconceivable, for instance, to think of being a slave trader. There the inconceivability arises because of the idea, and the fault is located there, so to speak. This is the case Berlin envisages.

However, it is also possible to envisage inconceivability arising because of the onlooker and some fault there. For example, a devout Nazi might indeed have found it inconceivable that Gentiles should pursue full equal civic rights for Jews as a goal in life. Such a person might well say, 'I cannot conceive what it would be like to pursue such a life.' At this stage in the argument, it is very far from clear that Berlin has given due weight to the point that his onlooker has a world-view and a nature, too, and that what is conceivable for someone is wedded to this nature and world-view.

The dangers of this are increased by the dramatic nature of Berlin's account. Once the point of inconceivability is reached, those holding the opinion or goal seem, on this line of argument, less than human: 'They are not human for me.' Yet twentieth-century history is tragically replete with examples of what human beings are capable of when they feel that another group, for reasons of race, religion or politics, can be classified as 'non-human'.

Fourth, the *former* part of the proposition, that humans have values, we fully affirm – in fact, some of the values Berlin and others endorse we endorse too, and happily. However, we distinguish between values that are purely human constructions and those that are divinely revealed in the Bible. This distinction means that in terms of the *latter* part of the proposition, that these values are at war, we concede that humanly constructed values may be at war both with each other and also with divinely revealed values. What we deny is that divinely revealed values are intrinsically at war with each other.

So the point at issue is *the relation that divinely revealed values bear to one another.*

The moral passion of Berlin's thesis

Two kinds of moral passion

There is no denying the moral passion with which Berlin pursues this idea of incommensurable pluralism. This passion arises from two considerations. First, Berlin sees this acceptance of incommensurable pluralism as undermining the impulse to various types of totalitarian or dictatorial action. It is precisely the idea of uniquely right answers that encourage the attitude that the ends justify the means. Berlin writes of the person who thinks that he or she has this unique answer:

> to make mankind just and happy and creative and harmonious for ever – what could be too high a price to pay for that? To make such an omelette, there is surely no limit to the number of eggs that should be broken – that was the faith of Lenin, of Trotsky, of Mao, for all I know of Pol Pot.[25]

But if one has lost the idea that one has the uniquely right answer to the human predicament, one loses the motivation for this kind of conduct. Berlin's impulse here is to support a humane liberalism.

The second way in which Berlin's moral passion emerges is over how one should hold one's values in this framework of incommensurable pluralism. Berlin's suggestion is not, he insists, an amoralism, where nothing is either right or wrong. It is a mistake to think that this kind of pluralist thought sees itself as endorsing no values. For Berlin, this is one of the crucial differences between incommensurable pluralism and 'relativism'.[26] 'Relativism' is identified by Berlin more with statements that are thought of essentially as only statements of personal preference, as in 'I like coffee, but you like tea.' These preferences do not have a moral flavour. Instead, Berlin envisages high degrees of morally based action. For the point is to live *as if* whatever ultimate value has

---

25. Berlin 1998a:13.
26. Berlin 1998a:9.

been selected really is ultimate: 'Principles are not less sacred because their duration cannot be guaranteed,' writes Berlin – we should still stand for them 'unflinchingly'.[27]

Let us pursue the moral ardour with which one stands for one's values in this system. In fact, we may stand for any given value *all the more unflinchingly*, because it is not commensurable with other values/virtues – it is 'free'; it is not necessarily regulated or mitigated by other values, for they are incommensurable. Take fox-hunting, for example. This really is not worth going to the stake for, either to ban or to protect it, because its value is not, indeed cannot, be set in any relation to other values. W. B. Yeats catches some of the consequences well when he speaks of a centreless world.[28]

In such a centreless world, which has no coordinated frame of reference, the problem is not that there are no values for us, but that virtues, in Chesterton's words, 'are isolated' from each other.[29] Yeats envisages two opposite consequences of this isolation. The first is a lack of conviction. For in incommensurable pluralism, who is to say that a particular value should prevail over others? Incommensurable pluralism may rob us of the ability to say one value or virtue should moderate or even overrule another. In some cases it can rob us of a sense of priority, even when there really is such a priority. The second is the passionate intensity with which some values are held. Perhaps it is not surprising that this is an age of many impassioned single-issue lobby groups, whether it is antivivisection, Fathers for Justice, or whatever. This is not to say these groups do not reflect or protect a virtue; but rather, it is a question of what relation these virtues bear to other virtues, whether a virtue is pursued with rightly proportioned passion.

Relating the two strands of Berlin's moral passion: a dilemma
There is, it seems to me, no doubting Berlin's moral seriousness on

27. Berlin 1998b:242.
28. W. B. Yeats, *The Second Coming*.
29. Chesterton 1909:51.

either of these two heads mentioned above. What is troubling is how the two interrelate. There seems to be a dilemma here.

For, on the one hand, let us suppose that I still hold my convictions and values with ultimate seriousness, standing for them 'unflinchingly' and treating them as still 'sacred'. If so, then what difference is there between that way of holding to those values which Berlin commends, and the way of holding which says, as in the model Berlin criticizes, that these are the uniquely right answers to the human problem? It appears that under both schemes values are held with equivalent passion, for that equivalence is Berlin's point. And if they are, then why should my holding my values as 'sacred' within incommensurable pluralism not produce the same results that Berlin fears in the 'monistic', one-right-answer, systems he castigates? But if one can 'unflinchingly' hold a value as 'sacred' without resorting to the most repellent kinds of coercion within the framework of incommensurable pluralism, then it does not seem necessarily impossible for those outside the framework of incommensurable pluralism likewise to be both morally passionate and unwilling to resort to coercion.

Yet if, on the other hand, Berlin were to concede that within incommensurable pluralism values are held as less sacred and not as unflinchingly, then his attempt to differentiate incommensurable pluralism from relativism looks correspondingly less successful, for the thrust of his distinction is that values are still held as more than purely personal preferences within incommensurable pluralism.

The application of incommensurable pluralism: the case of Machiavelli

It is also intriguing to see how Berlin develops this idea of incommensurable goods. As we have seen, he draws upon it in dealing with Machiavelli,[30] the famous, or notorious, writer of Renaissance

---

30. Berlin 1998c.

Florence. There are many interpretations of Machiavelli.[31] Berlin adds his own.

In Berlin's view, the thing is this: it is *not* that Machiavelli simply separates politics from ethics, rendering politics an 'ethics-free zone'. Machiavelli is not just an amoralist in politics. *Rather*, it is that Machiavelli recognizes two different *moral* systems. There is a Christian one ('not indeed, . . . defective in itself')[32] and a 'pagan' one. For Berlin, Machiavelli endorses both and applies, in politics, the 'pagan' one. Machiavelli is therefore a profoundly moral political writer, attempting to apply morality, not abolish it.

This is rather chilling: on the adoption of these 'pagan' virtues, which can necessitate deceit and political purges, Berlin notes that '[Machiavelli] calls for great sacrifices in their name'.[33] Indeed. However, on this take of Machiavelli, which is just where Berlin thinks Machiavelli is so good, those actions are morally justified. This must be stressed: the 'pagan' values cannot be criticized from within the Christian system because of the principle of incommensurability.

At this point, the comparative lack of a full account of human nature within this idea of incommensurable pluralism seems deeply disturbing. If humans are prone to producing moral rationalizations of their actions, finding ways in which they can describe any actions of theirs as morally justified, then the Berlin thesis provides a way of reinforcing this still further, for my rationalizations are still more immune to criticism. This, again, is not a recipe for less repressive actions in human life, but more. A Stalin will have further grounds for saying his purges are beyond reproach.[34] Berlin's thesis risks frustrating one of its primary goals, the restraint of tyranny.

---

31. Bernard Crick gives a lucid and brief account in his introduction to *The Discourses* (Machiavelli 1970), especially pp. 61–67 on the question of politics and morality.

32. Berlin 1998c:301.

33. Berlin 1998c:301.

34. For the tendency during Stalin's Terror to produce 'moral' justification see Conquest 1968.

Machiavelli's preferences

The Machiavelli example, however, reveals another problematic feature about the actual application of incommensurable pluralism. Let us suppose that Berlin is right and that Machiavelli does envisage two moral universes. The point is, he prefers one. What is more, his preference is not arbitrary, but reasoned: if one wishes to retain power, then this is what one must do. Yet here, of course, we find Machiavelli using a basis of comparison. Christian ethics and 'pagan' ones are compared on the basis of effective retention of power. But there is a basis of comparison. As such the two systems are clearly not incommensurable. Machiavelli himself does not seem to be, then, a simple incommensurable pluralist.

It is true that the two systems (in the way Machiavelli describes them) are not compatible, by which we mean that in certain given situations, say, over lying to the populace, the two different systems tell us to do different things and so produce two different results. But this does not mean they are necessarily incommensurable. The mere existence of incompatibility between moral values does not, by itself, tell us the systems are incommensurable.

This difference between incommensurability and incompatibility needs some explanation. Some things may indeed be incompatible because they are incommensurable. However, incompatibility may arise for other reasons: one value may have no objective justification, and exists purely as a product of human imagination, while the other may be rooted in the will of God for his creatures. Incompatibility there may arise because of the sinful defiance by humans of their Creator. Incompatibility may also arise when two values, rooted in the will of God for his creatures, are imperfectly understood by those creatures. Thus a promise to give to charity may conflict with a duty to support one's family.[35] Here the duties of truthfulness and love of family apparently conflict. But this may be because we do not fully understand the scope of either duty.

To adopt the terminology of jurisprudence for a moment, the

---

35. An example cited by Williams (1979), who sympathizes with Berlin's thesis.

norms are imperfectly individuated; that is to say, the content of
the rules is not set out with perfect precision. For instance, our
competence to make promises to bind ourselves may be limited.
English law recognizes this, of course, with its idea that one
cannot make a contract by which one sells oneself into slavery.

Yet Berlin's thesis tends to obscure the fact that we do have
preferences between goals, and we think these preferences are
rational. Such preferences imply commensurability of some sort.
At this point we perhaps should recognize more strongly the
role of these preferences and why they should be laid open to
scrutiny. After all, Berlin himself prefers his system of incommensurable pluralism to earlier ideas of a unified moral universe,
and it would be a great disservice to him to say this preference
was arbitrary. His choice is a reasoned one based on what he sees
as incoherence and a tendency to justify tyranny. But if Berlin is
right and incommensurable pluralism is true, so that one cannot
properly, rationally, compare one moral universe with another,
why should I anyway prefer incommensurable pluralism to any
other moral universe?

We must, then, note some key points. First, Berlin gives us a
strongly moral framework in this kind of pluralism. Second, the
cardinal values that we have adopted in Berlin's system enjoy a
freedom from criticism. Why? because alternative values have
been weeded out, and put in another 'incommensurable' system.
One does not have to listen to the criticism implied by an alternative value, because – the apples and oranges principle – one cannot
compare the two. Hence one's first principle operates intact and
unrestrained. Third, there is a real question of selectivity. Berlin
tells us about several incommensurable systems. Which system
applies when? And who says? Fourth, Berlin's system can be as
readily appropriated by tyrants as the ones he criticizes, possibly
even more so.

Theological evaluation

After this description of, and brief comment on, incommensurable pluralism we must proceed to a more specifically theological

evaluation. We shall do this under two main headings: evaluation in relation to God, and in relation to humans.

In relation to God . . .

Incommensurable pluralism implicitly denies things about God. It is worth here distinguishing two different ways that discussion of values can affect our understanding of God. We might mean by 'values' what God wills for human beings: how he has decreed we should live our lives. We might also mean by 'values' qualities or aspects of God's own nature. Incommensurable pluralism

- first, is polytheist, so it denies biblical monotheism; and
- second, deals in incommensurable plurality so it denies God's simplicity.

Let us develop these in turn.

Polytheism

As we consider the constellations of incommensurable values, we should realize they bear many of the hallmarks of polytheism. After all, those values are in practice treated as ultimate and they are discrete and incommensurable. That there is no overall order is, one might say, the whole point. One goes from one to another. But it is just here that there are echoes of the fractured, localized polytheism of 1 Kings 20:23 and 2 Kings 17:26, where gods compete with each other in no particular order, and there is no genuinely overarching value or god. In contrast, passages like Isaiah 40:18–31 show God alone is incomparable as Sovereign and Creator of all.

The regime that Berlin describes is polycratic – polycratic in that there are many competing centres of power and authority. For Berlin this stands in opposition to 'monism',[36] where things can be reduced to an integrated single moral universe.

In fact, it is enormously difficult to integrate this incommensurable pluralism into a truly monotheistic framework. It is worth

---

36. A key idea in both Berlin 1998b and Berlin 1998c.

here recalling some earlier ideas about monotheism. It was common Patristic and Reformation ground that monotheism goes hand in hand with cosmic monarchy. It is especially an Athanasian idea.[37] On this view, monotheism indicates a supreme being with cosmic monarchy and order. There is an interrelation of parts, both physically and ethically. They fit together, and this causes no surprise, since they are products from nothing of the Creator, and are sustained by his single will and mind. There is one unified cosmos because there is one single Creator.

So the pattern tends to be *monotheism implies cosmic monarchy, which in its turn implies ordered relations within the cosmos.* All very well, someone might reply, but could there be a biblical monotheism where God willed mutually contradictory and incommensurable virtues? We need to be clear about what this would involve. First, this would not be a case of so-called conflict between God's permissive and decretive wills, because in that way of putting things there is ultimate resolution. Second, this is not a case of bringing good out of an evil action, because again there is a single integrated end in mind. Rather, the issue is this: that at the same level of willing there are two ends equally willed. At this point God's relation to the world is very definitely not that of a monarch whose plan ultimately comes to fruition (Eph. 1:11): it cannot be, because there are several plans or purposes for him at the same level of willing. Even if only one thing happens, other equally willed things do not. To that extent, the idea that God wills two contradictory values or virtues for us and for us to act upon eliminates the idea of biblical monarchy. It also eliminates the idea of sin, although this is another point.

I should add that texts about double-mindedness on God's part do not in fact constitute exceptions to this, given that they are accommodated to us and our place within time.[38]

This question of plural, contradictory wills in God affects our consideration of plural gospels. For the gospel is not just a communication of information, a newsflash to an otherwise unin-

---

37. Especially Athanasius, *Contra Gentes* 6.
38. Texts cited in this connection include Jon. 4:2 and 1 Kgs 21:29.

formed world. It is a command by God to his human creatures and requires their obedience. Thus in 2 Thessalonians 1:8, disobeying the gospel is a ground for punishment (see also 1 Pet. 4:17). The gospel is something that God wills men and women to believe. This means that plural, in the sense of incommensurably different and incompatible, gospels involve God willing different and incompatible things. As we have seen, this kind of incompatible willing by God cannot be reconciled with his divine monarchy. Hence incommensurably different and incompatible gospels cannot be reconciled with God's monarchy.

Denial of simplicity

Let us move to our second denial, the denial of simplicity. Simplicity is a term that is perhaps less familiar to us as evangelicals these days than was once the case. To say that God is simple is not saying that God is somehow simple-minded, or that he is a primitive prototype as against later and more advanced models. To say that God is simple is to say, first, that in God, all his attributes are essential. There are no optional extras in God, something added on to the basic product. So, a car might have air conditioning. If air conditioning is a secondary characteristic, a particular car, a particular model, a particular colour, might be available without the air conditioning. But with God, it is not the case that there are add-on extras, as if his justice was something that was an optional extra with him, which could be taken away and he would still be the same essential being. Rather, take away the justice and he is no longer the God of the Bible. It is not the case with God that some attributes are primary, some secondary.

The reason why this matters is that if we did have a God with primary and secondary attributes, we would always be tempted to downplay the attributes we felt less comfortable with to secondary attributes. So, it is wonderful to say God is love, but it would be wrong to say that other things such as holiness are somehow less important to him. Simplicity minimizes the designer-deity tendency humans have, the urge to pick and mix the attributes we personally like best.

Second, simplicity means that all God's attributes are integrated. God is not a mixture or composition of more basic principles, into which he can be divided. As all the attributes are equally essential, so all the attributes are inseparable. So, going back to Chesterton's remarks, with God, because he is simple, his truth is pitying, and his pity is truthful.

The great, the fantastic, thing that earlier generations emphasized about God's simplicity was that it supports, perhaps even entails, his faithfulness to his promises. There is no other conflicting attribute in God that will prevent him from fulfilling his promise to have mercy on those who believe in the Lord Jesus, for instance.

We see this biblically in Psalm 85:10–13. Consider verse 10, for instance: *Righteousness and peace kiss.* The image is of justice (*righteousness*) and salvation attributes (*peace*) meeting and being reconciled. Please note, they are not set in conflict – one does not trump the other, they are not traded off so one gets a little bit of righteousness and a little bit of peace. The language is of both being fully present and realized, and in harmony, not as incommensurables, nor irreconcilables. Perhaps even more strikingly, in the New Testament we could cite Romans 3:25–26, where the point is that God's forbearance is not at odds with his own righteousness.

So simplicity means we cannot set God's attributes in opposition to each other: his is a pitying truth and a truthful pity. William Ames (1576–1633) catches it well: 'the divine attributes are not contrary to one another, but agree emphatically'.[39] This also means we cannot prioritize one of God's attributes as '*the* essential' attribute of God.

The instability of incommensurable pluralism
However, we also need to see how the Church Fathers in particular saw polytheism developing. For they did not envisage polytheism with its polycratic emphases as a stable system.

Remember that Athanasius argued

No monarchy → no God[40]

---

39. Ames 1997:I.iv.23
40. *Contra Gentes* 6.

God's cosmic sovereignty is not something that is an optional extra for God. Rather, if we deny God's cosmic sovereignty, this entails 'atheism', in the sense that there is no god who answers the biblical description of the word.

Gregory of Nazianzus, one of the Cappadocian Fathers who succeeded Athanasius, continues and develops this. He sees three basic alternatives: monarchy, polyarchy and anarchy.[41] But he adds this twist. He thinks ultimately polyarchy becomes anarchy, so that finally there are two alternatives: monarchy or anarchy. That alternative of monarchy or anarchy is ultimately related to the alternative: monotheism or 'atheism'. After all, as we've seen in this line of thought, monotheism goes hand in hand with monarchy, and atheism is the denial of monotheism and therefore of monarchy.

This sounds merely theoretical, but we should think it through more concretely. What happens in anarchy? Why do we fear it so much in some respects? Well, because things are decided on the basis of might is right. Might acts unrestrained by principle or law. In anarchy, by definition, you do not get the rule of law. This absence of law and principle does not just arise in so-called primitive societies. We might well in a Western context speak of the 'tyranny of the majority' as anarchistic. 'Tyranny of the majority' is Alexis de Tocqueville's pungent phrase for describing how in a democratic society the majority can behave tyrannically, because the majority reserve the prerogative to redefine right to suit themselves.[42] The example de Tocqueville cites for this is the expropriation of native American lands by 'due' legislative and judicial process. Is not tyranny of the majority an apt phrase for what happened in Rocco's case? That his rights, theoretically guaranteed by the European Convention, scarcely even rated a mention, while the media was full of the rights of those who wanted to deny him his?

And in this anarchistic world, an unbelieving majority will feel itself entitled to disenfranchise messages and beliefs of which it

---

41. *Third Oration on the Son* 1f.

42. De Tocqueville (1805–59) was a French politician/writer best known for *Democracy in America*.

strongly disapproves. However, in the case of the gospel, this feeling of entitlement will be married to a basic antipathy to the gospel message. This could well create a profound temptation, even an inevitable tendency, to disenfranchise proclamation of the gospel itself. In the light of that, it is important to see how the feeling of entitlement arises, as I have done here.

Lastly, in this anarchistic world, one of the regularities that disappears is God's faithfulness. After all, if a promise made with one thing in view is subject to competing values that may master or frustrate it, how can promises be sure?

The gospel of Christ

What does this mean, then, for the proclamation of the gospel? First, it highlights the centrality of proclaiming a kingdom, a monarchy, in particular the monarchy or kingdom of Jesus, for it is on him that the Father has bestowed the kingdoms of the world: Psalm 2:8. We should add that this is how Jesus himself understands matters. He states that the Father has given him all authority (John 17:2, before the passion and Matt. 28:18 after the passion). We have already seen how kingdom or monarchy is inseparable from the biblical God who is Creator of all, seen and unseen. If we have a gospel that sacrifices the idea of God's monarchy, vested in his Son, then this is not the monotheistic biblical God of the Bible. It is, of course, for just this reason that the chapters in this book inevitably deal with the idea of kingdom in one way or another. A gospel featuring the biblical God inevitably deals, expressly or by necessary implication, with his kingdom or his monarchy.

Followers of Berlin might feel some misgivings at this point. Berlin understandably voices suspicion of those who go to extreme lengths to fulfil their monolithic utopian vision, whatever it may be. Recall the sentiment noted earlier: 'To make such an omelette [A perfect society], there is surely no limit to the number of eggs that should be broken – that was the faith of Lenin, of Trotsky, of Mao, for all I know of Pol Pot.'[43]

However, followers of Jesus Christ note this difference in the

---

43. Berlin 1998a:13.

kingdom of Christ. Where Lenin made his omelette by breaking others, Jesus gives his own body to be broken. Characteristic evangelical presentations of the gospel stress precisely the finished nature of Christ's work and its sufficiency, focused on the idea that salvation is by grace alone and not by human works. In this sense, the content of the gospel itself, as the message that the king has died for his people, is at odds with the fears that Berlin has: for those fears relate to what humans must do to construct their heaven on earth. Put another way, Berlin's argument has not grasped that the kingdom of Christ is constructed by his work and sacrifice, not ours.

Second, our gospel involves proclaiming a simple God, in the way that I have explained simplicity. We deal with the Jesus in whom God's one plan for salvation is fulfilled in human history – we do not meet God pursuing incommensurable goals; and to that extent we have to recognize how 'un-gospel' the sentiments of incommensurable pluralism are, even when some of the values one finds (such as the importance of the individual, the antipathy to tyranny) are ones with which we agree.

This is undoubtedly complex, because it leaves us needing to distinguish between our agreement on the point that individuals matter and our disagreement about the context in which that point is set. However, this offers an opportunity, too, for we may rightly argue that these legitimate values can be properly supported only from within a biblical framework. For example, that respect for other humans finds its best basis in biblical understandings of human beings as creatures made in the image of God. This is, of course, strongly present in the presuppositional apologetics of Cornelius Van Til and others.

Third, we must turn to the cross, so frequently the focus of evangelical presentations of the gospel. The cross is naturally at the heart of gospel proclamations, because it is about the kingdom of God, as judgment executed on sin, vindicating God's sovereignty. We must recall that the cross does not take place because of miscalculation or accident, but by God's set plan and foreknowledge (Acts 2:23). Note too the Johannine stress on the fulfilment of prophecy in the crucifixion, and Jesus' explanation of the prophets on the road to Emmaus (Luke 24:26f). In that way the cross is a testimony to God's sovereignty, but it is also a testimony to God's simplicity. This must be stressed. The cross is a case, perhaps the case par excellence, where several attributes are simultaneously perfectly satisfied: notably, justice and mercy meet.

This reconciling of justice and mercy is especially striking in the context of this discussion, since the irreconcilable conflict of justice and mercy is an example of incommensurability cited by those persuaded by Berlin's thesis: their point is that justice and mercy do not meet.[44] Instead, so the reasoning runs, there are two choices before us in situations where justice and mercy both apply. We can opt for one or the other and have it perfectly, in which case the other may not be realized even imperfectly. Alternatively, we can choose to have imperfect justice and imperfect mercy, but, stresses the Berlin line of thought, we should acknowledge the imperfection.

However, the Bible presents us with a God who is both just and merciful. This is evident from the key theophany of Exodus 34:5ff, where God reveals his character both in terms of his mercy (Exod. 34:6) and his justice (necessarily implicit in the phrasing about not clearing the guilty: Exod. 34:7). God's commitment to justice emerges in the history of Israel and Judah. Thus in Amos chapters 1 and 2, God decrees merited punishment on the Gentile nations surrounding the kingdoms of Israel and Judah. These decrees are, of course, expressed in a repeated formula: 'for three transgressions of [whichever city or kingdom] and for four, I will not turn away the punishment . . . because . . . [and then a clause specifying the crimes committed]'. The formulaic expressions Amos employs here stress both that the actions about which God complains are sin or crime and also that his reactions are morally merited responses to what has been done. However, an obvious feature of justice is that similar crimes deserve similar treatment. As such, given the commitment to justice shown in the condemnation on Gentiles by Amos 1:3 – 2:3, it is no surprise to find a just God likewise stipulating judgment on Judah (Amos 2:4–5) and Israel (Amos 2:6ff).

---

44. See e.g. Williams 1979. Berlin and his followers are frequently more concerned, though, with a different value conflict: that between freedom and equality.

Other pre-exilic prophets, like Isaiah and Jeremiah, provide further examples of God's commitment to justice, even when that involves the execution of justice on his covenant people. In addition, we should note the way that the post-exilic penitential prayers of Nehemiah (e.g. Neh. 9:33) and Daniel (e.g. Dan. 9:7 and 14) alike feature confessions of God's justice and covenant faithfulness and consistency in bringing the exile on Israel and Judah. At this point it is evident that the justice of God is a perilous thing for men and women who have failed to live by his word. Justice becomes simultaneously something to be desired and to be avoided.

Yet the same material also contains promises by this promise-keeping God that he will show mercy. Thus Amos 9:11–15 closes with predictions of mercy and favour to the people who have deserved judgment. Likewise, the prayers of Ezra (Ezra 9) and Daniel (Dan. 9, especially at v. 18) appeal to God's mercy. These prayers are perhaps particularly striking: there seems no sense of appealing to an inconsistent attribute of God in appealing to his mercy. Rather, there is a consciousness that God is faithful to his word and that the exile shows precisely this (Neh. 9:29–30, 33–35; and Dan. 9:12–13). And it is just this consistency and faithfulness to his word that prompts Daniel's prayer in the first place and on which he relies, as he contemplates the promises made through Jeremiah (Dan. 9:2–3).[45]

Several responses are possible as we regard this presence of both mercy and justice in the biblical material. We could, of course, simply deem the two as inconsistent and privilege one strand or the other. There are traces of such an attitude in those who deny Amos 9:11–15 is authentic. For them the discrepancy between those verses and the bulk of the rest of the book is too great – they are incommensurable, and we should, the argument runs, accept that Amos's 'real' message is the message of destructive justice on sinful people, whether Israelite or Gentile. This approach reveals a trajectory or tendency, the tendency to put one's message, one's gospel, in terms of either justice or mercy.

---

45. Compare Neh. 9:31 for a similar point regarding God's pre-exilic actions.

Arguably, some presentations of the gospel today risk doing just that: that mercy is proffered in our gospel talks without due consideration of the justice of God (Bonhoeffer's criticism of 'cheap grace' still merits attention). Similarly, understandable passions for justice, especially social justice, sometimes sound as though there is no prospect of mercy for some, notably the rich, for wealth is, it seems, for some, the new unforgivable sin.

Yet in fact the presence side by side of mercy and justice is quite central to the Old Testament presentation of God. As well as the theophany of Exodus 34, key material in Deuteronomy, especially chapters 28–30, deals both with God's inevitable justice (e.g. Deut. 28:15–68) and his mercy (e.g. Deut. 30:3ff). The emphasis of Amos, Isaiah and Jeremiah on both justice and mercy is therefore typical of this covenantal outlook.

Moreover, the reality of Israel's Old Testament experience shows all too painfully that human beings stand in need of both justice and mercy. A gospel without perfect justice entails us in a future that falls short of perfect justice. Berlin is quite right here that if one does really think values are incommensurable, then some or all of them will not be perfectly realized. Similarly, a gospel without perfect mercy is actually a gospel without hope for a human race that has universally, with the exception of Jesus, fallen into sin.

Yet in the cross, God's just wrath against sinners is perfectly met. For judgment on sin is executed. In that sense, the cross is not a triumph of God's mercy in which justice is displaced and the need to administer it somehow ignored. Nor is the cross a triumph of justice which precludes mercy, for the cross is the supreme act of mercy, as well as an act of justice. There, undeservedly, the Son of God took my place, the place which morally I did deserve, and in his great love endured in the stead of sinners like me the wrath that would otherwise directly fall on us. This remains an act directed to me and my sin since by faith-union I am united to Christ. One of the results of this faith-union is that just as he is clothed in our sin, so we are clothed in his righteousness. But as he becomes sin for our sakes and in union with us, the just penalty for sin is observed. As he becomes sin for our sakes undeservedly and out of his gracious love for us, his mercy is manifest.

The penal substitutionary death of the Son, in pursuit of a single promised plan for redemption spanning human history (1 Pet. 1:20), is really a testimony amongst other things to the simplicity of God, in whom all attributes are perfectly realized, without trade-off or competition or compromise. Considered in this light, the penal substitutionary death of the cross is part and parcel of the sovereign and simple God. Indeed, without it, there is no little difficulty in formulating an account of redemption that does not sacrifice either God's mercy or his justice. The penal substitutionary view of the cross underlines the moral coherence of the universe, not its incommensurable values.

In short, we may say the cross is plural, yet unified, and perhaps the greatest criticism we could launch against Berlin's incommensurable pluralism is that it is not cross-shaped.

It is said above that the cross is plural, in that it shows both justice and mercy perfectly realized. That takes us to the point that Christians do not necessarily deny plurality and diversity in the affairs of the cosmos, even though the Bible teaches the uniqueness of God and his sole monarchy. But just as Paul spoke about a better way, so perhaps we should speak of a better pluralism. By this I mean a pluralism that is ultimately coherent and commensurable, while Berlin's is incommensurable and ultimately breeds incoherence. Just as an incommensurable pluralism denies sovereignty and simplicity, so a Christ-based pluralism will affirm precisely sovereignty and simplicity.

However, we must note how it is that we are integrating, co-ordinating and rendering commensurable the diverse actions and values that human life contains: through Christ's lordship. In some respects, this principle is already recognized amongst us in our corporate life as Christ's church. We are rightly used to the idea of diversity of gifts and ministry within the church, but nevertheless we are instructed to have an orderly diversity, with an integrating principle, the edification of Christ's people under his lordship (see 1 Cor. 12 – 14). We should not, therefore, find principles of co-ordination or uniformity simply arbitrarily imposed by humans.

Yet are there not some obvious extensions to these arguments? Those same arguments about sovereignty and coherence under Christ apply with equal force more widely than the life of the church. If we are serious that the gospel involves God's kingdom realized through his Son, then the ambit of that kingdom should not be arbitrarily restricted by human decision. There is a real question to face, whether we have done something like this in our comparative slowness, within the context of English evangelicalism, to apply Christ's sovereignty to literature, or the visual or cinematic arts, or the sciences. What it is to write a Christian piece of literature or do biology in a way that upholds Christ's lordship is certainly an unfamiliar, indeed unfashionable, question, given its association with that slightly unfashionable Dutchman, Abraham Kuyper.[46] Yet defending the gospel against the claims of ideas such as Berlin's incommensurable pluralism seems to take us back to just this place.

After all, if we fail to do this we run the risk if instating a new kind of incommensurable pluralism, one where there is a realm where Christ is rightly Lord, the world of the believer and the church; there, one set of rules and expectations applies. But there would also be other realms where different rules and expectations apply. This may well be how some Christians in the United Kingdom have at times behaved, comparatively reluctant to engage in the public forum, and with a tendency to leave matters of faith as essentially private. Yet it is hard to see how this differs in effect from incommensurable pluralism, and this, as we have seen, is an implicit denial of the kingdom of Christ.

In relation to humans . . .
We should move now to think of incommensurable pluralism in relation to humans. Perhaps the first thing to strike us here is the relationship with idolatry.

Idolatry
The reason why incommensurable pluralism takes us back to idolatry is that incommensurable pluralism seems inevitably to involve

---

46. Kuyper's case for the universal lordship of Christ applying to all the spheres of human conduct, not just the life of the church, is set out concisely in his *Lectures on Calvinism*.

a very strong element of human sovereignty. In incommensurable pluralism we have values or virtues that govern our lives, and the values are ones that we each select, arranged as we want, just as in idolatry we shape whichever gods we have chosen to our own specifications. More than this, we should note how we become invulnerable to criticism. The invulnerability comes from the way values, and hence value-systems, are incommensurable. If they are incommensurable, then you cannot employ your values to criticize the values others have chosen, for your values *belong* in a different set from those other values. Your criticism will be met with the response that it does not apply, because it would be like comparing apples with oranges. In that respect, the former Bishop of Edinburgh, Richard Holloway, affords a good example of this invulnerability to criticism as he utilizes Berlin's ideas of incommensurability to fireproof his defence of practising homosexuality from objections.[47] We should remember, too, that this process renders evangelism impossible to defend, because one cannot categorize the values others hold as idolatry, from which they should turn to serve the true and living God (1 Thess. 1:9).

In this context, it is relevant to recall the account that Tertullian, the redoubtable Church Father, provides of idolatry.[48] He points out that idolatry arises with perilous ease when real values are valued, but valued to the exclusion of others. For then indeed something of genuine value can stand in God's place, excluding God and obstructing proper sight of him.[49] That value can exclude the true biblical picture of God, in whom all the genuine values are coherently found. Chesterton saw the tragedy of this with exceptional clarity in the passage we have already quoted. The point is not that the virtues to which Chesterton refers are not real virtues, established by God. The point is that, shorn of their true integration in the one God, they function as idols. Indeed, the very fact that they do have an origin in God's ordained scale of values

---

47. Lecture at Middlesex University, 1998.

48. Fl. AD. 200 Tertullian wrote in Latin and lived in Carthage, in modern-day Tunisia.

49. *Pro deo adversus deum.*

can give them a tremendous plausibility, as C. S. Lewis rightly sees in *The Great Divorce*, where he discusses how divinely willed virtues can become all the more terrible as idols, because they are great virtues.

It is difficult, finally, to ignore some of the more pastoral issues idolatry tends to create. Idolatry (which is described in Hosea chapters 1 and 2 as a 'whoredom') parodies proper spiritual marriage, just as adultery parodies legitimate marriage. The Bible notes our tendency to become like our idols (Ps. 115:8, for example). We should here recall that we analysed incommensurable pluralism earlier as polytheist, with, in fact, a tendency to cosmic anarchy. What would that mean for people who live and 'worship' (in the sense of ascribing great worth) within that world-view? If this analysis of polytheism is correct, it would not be entirely surprising if it did not produce 'disintegrated' humans; that is to say, humans who miss any final integration within themselves – humans who have no centre, to use again the language of Yeats's poem. In the light of this, it is no cause for amazement that human urban life in the West is so marked by inconsistency and lacunae: our culture has come to love its private versus public distinctions, with different rules for each; we have come to thrive on differential application of norms, permitting things for one group while denying them for another. No-one, for instance, will be holding their breath to wait for pro-homosexual activists to be prosecuted under Britain's law-and-order legislation in the way Harry Hammond was.

The appeal to self-righteousness: hypocrisy

This survey of our tendency to idolatry needs, perhaps, to be considered in conjunction with another feature of the biblical description of humans. The Bible tells us that humans are not simply given to wrongdoing while overtly acknowledging their wrongness. We are not in the habit of raising our hands and confessing, 'We quite see that we're doing wrong and intend to go on doing what we know is morally indefensible.' Rather, we harbour a strong streak of hypocrisy – a tendency to do wrong things while simultaneously asserting our moral rectitude. Thus John 16:1ff features Jesus' foretelling that the disciples will be persecuted: this is not done because of a freely confessed hatred of God; rather, it is done while – terribly – claiming to be loyal to God. The reality, though, as Jesus makes clear in the surrounding material, is one of hatred of God and his anointed (John 15:23–24; 16:3). In a similar way, the final result that Paul describes in the downward spiral of sin in Romans 1:18–32 comes in verse 32 where Paul describes not a simple amoralism, where nothing is right or wrong, but an inverted moralism, where what is wrong has been called right.

Incommensurable pluralism needs to be related to this streak of hypocrisy. We have stressed above that incommensurable pluralism in effect allows us to pick our supreme values, because it allows us to see values in splendid isolation from each other, permitting them to be secure from criticism and competition. If we do indeed have a tendency to hypocrisy, this is like leaving a gin bottle in front of an alcoholic, because we shall be inclined to choose our values in ways that guarantee our rightness and also our immunity. As such, incommensurable pluralism allows, dare one say it fosters, moral opportunism and hypocrisy: it allows the luxury of a self-indulgence that also rejoices in its moral self-righteousness. But perhaps that has become merely descriptive of much of contemporary Britain.

Conclusions

We therefore conclude: first, Berlin's incommensurable pluralism itself runs the risk of incoherence and can give rise to the very thing Berlin so fears, a ruthless and unaccountable tyranny and, despite its good intentions, the erosion of civic liberties.

As such, second, we must indeed go on looking for and proclaiming 'the' gospel. Looking for 'the' gospel implies singularity and coherence. This is quite compatible with recognizing plurality and diversity, but not compatible with a particular type of pluralism: incommensurable pluralism. This matters because the gospel is a question of obedience and God's will for our lives. An inconsistent series of gospels means God has inconsistent wills for us.

Third, we need to recognize that such incommensurable pluralism is polytheistic, and if we were to accept this kind of pluralism, whether tacitly or explicitly, we would by implication be denying something: we would be denying God's monarchy, and God's simplicity. In short, we would have a different god. We would also be rendering ourselves even more vulnerable than we already are to some remarkable temptations: a temptation to idolatry and a temptation to hypocrisy.

This means that when we do encounter claims that a particular 'gospel proclamation' is drawing out another different strand of gospel teaching, we need to exercise considerable care as to whether this different kerygma or proclamation represents a diversity that is coherent or incoherent, commensurable or incommensurable. Where the diversity remains coherent, and the biblical foundation justified, we must joyfully admit the diversity, for it enriches our understanding of God's way with his world. Where the diversity becomes incoherent, then justifications arising from diversity and potential for enrichment cannot succeed.

Fourth, this survey of incommensurable pluralism takes us back to a sharp focus on the cross of Jesus Christ, and a renewed wonder at it, because it represents not the imperfection of values in God's plan of salvation or their incommensurability, but precisely their commensurability, as justice and mercy meet and are equally perfected, so that with God there is a just mercy and a merciful justice. Here, incommensurable pluralism signally fails to explain who God is, and what he has done for our salvation.

© Michael Ovey, 2006.

2. 'KINGDOM OF GOD' AND 'ETERNAL LIFE' IN THE SYNOPTIC GOSPELS AND JOHN

Paul Woodbridge

Introduction

John's Gospel – what a great Gospel! If you really want to understand Jesus and why he came, this is the Gospel to read. Someone has described the remarkable nature of this Gospel by saying that it is a book in which 'a child can wade and an elephant can swim'.[1] So a first-time reader of John finds it clear, and understands what it is saying about Jesus Christ in a straightforward, yet profound, manner, while someone who has been studying John for many years can still be wrestling with its symbolic language and numerous nuances, and seeing increasing depths on each reading.[2]

But it is when one begins to consider the Fourth Gospel alongside the Synoptic Gospels that various contrasts present themselves. In the second century, Clement of Alexandria called John 'the spiritual Gospel', in contrast with the other Gospels

---

1. This description is noted by Morris 1995:3.

2. See also the comments of Kysar 1975:6.

which set out 'the outward (physical) facts'.[3] And it was the view of John Calvin that

> the other three are more copious in their narrative of the life and death of Christ, but John dwells more largely on the doctrine by which the office of Christ, together with the power of his death and resurrection, is unfolded . . . The doctrine which points out to us the power and benefit of the coming of Christ, is far more clearly exhibited by John than by the rest. And . . . the former three exhibit his body, if we may be permitted to use the expression, but John exhibits his soul. On this account, I am accustomed to say that this Gospel is a key to open the door for understanding the rest.[4]

It almost seems that when we read the Fourth Gospel after reading the first three, we are entering a different atmosphere, a different type of world. It is in any case a fact that only about 8% of John's content is paralleled in the Synoptics; that is, about 92% of his material is unique to John.

There certainly seem to be a number of differences between them.[5]

Material omitted by the Fourth Gospel
Much material found in the Synoptics is omitted in the Fourth Gospel, such as the exorcisms, lepers being healed, mention of the Sadducees, Jesus' baptism, the call of the Twelve, the transfiguration, the temptation narrative and the Sermon on the Mount.

Material found only in the Fourth Gospel
By contrast, material unique to the Fourth Gospel includes that found in chapters 2–4, the raising of Lazarus (ch. 11), the foot-

---

3. As quoted in Eusebius, *Hist. eccl.* 6.14.7, cited by Borchert 1996:89.
4. Calvin 1959:6.
5. For detailed discussion of Johannine distinctives as well as similarities, and ways of interpreting the various differences, see especially Blomberg 1987:153–159; 2001a:73–77; 2001b. See also www.bible.org, 'Major Differences between John and the Synoptics', by W. Hall Harris III.

washings (ch. 13), the farewell discourse (chs. 14–17) and Jesus' conversation with Pilate (18:28ff).

Differences in chronology

Much of Jesus' ministry in the Fourth Gospel is in Jerusalem, while in the Synoptics he goes to Jerusalem only near the end of his life. The cleansing of the temple occurs at the start of the Fourth Gospel, but towards the end of Jesus' life in the Synoptics. Jesus' anointing takes place prior to the triumphal entry in the Fourth Gospel (John 12:1–8, 12–15), but compare Matthew 26:6–13, 21:4–9, where it occurs afterwards. The Last Supper seems to have been eaten 24 hours earlier in the Fourth Gospel compared to the Synoptics, before the Passover, with crucifixion happening the day after (Thursday).

'High' Christology

Jesus is acknowledged as Messiah at the start of the Fourth Gospel! There seems to be a gradual development in the Synoptics. Yet examining John 1:29, 34, 36, 41, 45, 49 (with John the Baptist, Andrew, Philip and Nathanael all acknowledging Jesus to be the Messiah), the 'higher' categories appear much earlier, and the Johannine Jesus 'bestrides the stage of history like some sort of colossus or deity'.[6] Some would also say that this Gospel is the only one that identifies Jesus directly as divine (cf. 1:1; 10:30; 20:28).

Presentation and content of Jesus' teaching[7]

At the risk of oversimplification, we note a contrast between the Synoptics and the Fourth Gospel in the way Jesus' teaching is presented, as well as in its content:

---

6. Cited by Witherington 1995:22ff, from Käsemann 1968: 22f.

7. For these tables and further discussion, see Dunn 1985:32–35.

Jesus' teaching	Synoptic Gospels	John
Style	Sayings, parables	Long discourses
Content	Kingdom of God	Jesus himself
	Little about himself	Little about the kingdom

We note particularly how often the word 'kingdom' is used by Jesus in the Synoptics and its comparative infrequency in the Fourth Gospel, and how often Jesus uses 'I' to refer to himself in John compared to the other Gospels:

	Matt.	Mark	Luke	John
Kingdom	47	18	37	5
'I'	17	9	10	118[8]

If one were to ask how often Jesus speaks of God as his Father in the four Gospels, again some statistics are revealing:

	Mark	Q[9]	Luke	Matt.	John
'Father'	3	4	4	31	100+
'the Father'	1	1	2	1	73[10]

It may be said that when one compares what is said about Christ in the Synoptics and John, it is like comparing a *photograph* of Jesus to a *portrait*, or even, as Dunn puts it, that the Synoptics give us a

---

8. Dunn 1985:34.

9. 'Q' refers to material common to both Matthew and Luke.

10. Dunn 1985:44.

portrait of Jesus, while the Fourth Gospel is more like an *impressionist painting*.[11] Both show us the real Jesus, but in a very different manner.

For the purpose of this chapter, I shall focus on the comparison between the use of the terms 'kingdom of God' and 'eternal life'. The emphasis on the kingdom of God found in the Synoptics is largely missing in John; the phrase 'kingdom of God' occurs only twice in John's Gospel (3:3, 5), and the noun 'kingdom' alone only three times (all in 18:36). Instead, we find John's emphasis on 'eternal life' as a present reality (John 5:24 etc.). At least statistically, the emphasis on 'eternal life' in John's Gospel is closer to the letters of Paul than to the Synoptic Gospels, as the following chart shows:[12]

	Life	Kingdom
Matt.	7	55
Mark	4	20
Luke	5	46
John	36	5
Acts	8	8
Paul's letters	37	14
John's letters	13	0
Rev.	23	9

So what does John mean by emphasizing 'eternal life' in his Gospel? Does it have any relationship to the Synoptics' emphasis on the kingdom of God? Or are these two different concepts, at the very least emphasizing two different things?

---

11. Dunn 1985:43.

12. Adapted from www.bible.org, a study by W. Hall Harris III, 'Background to the Study of John'.

Consideration of John 3:3, 5 and 18:36

As the only cases of 'the kingdom of God' in the Fourth Gospel occur in 3:3, 5, and the only occurrences of 'kingdom' occur in 18:36, it is necessary to consider these verses, evaluate their meaning and the reason the term is used, as well as possible overlap with the Synoptics. It is also necessary to consider why 'kingdom of God' occurs so little in the Fourth Gospel in contrast to its frequency in the other Gospels.

Shared traditions

We may observe a point of shared traditions between the Synoptics and the Fourth Gospel in the Johannine language of 'seeing' or 'entering' the kingdom of God, in 3:3, 5. A number of Synoptic texts also speak of 'entering' the kingdom. See, for instance, Matthew 5:20 ('For I tell you, unless your righteousness exceeds that of the scribes and Pharisees, you will never enter the kingdom of heaven'); Matthew 7:21 ('Not everyone who says to me, "Lord, Lord", will enter the kingdom of heaven'); and see also Matthew 18:3 and Mark 10:23–25. Further, 'seeing' the kingdom may be compared with Mark 9:1 ('And he said to them, "Truly, I say to you, there are some standing here who will not taste death until they see the kingdom of God after it has come with power"') and Luke 13:28 ('see Abraham . . . in the kingdom of God').[13]

John 3:3, 5

In John 3, Jesus is approached by 'a man of the Pharisees', who makes an apparently flattering and implicitly believing statement – Jesus is a teacher from God, since he does various signs. However, Jesus seems to understand this greeting as a question concerning what he (Nicodemus) must do to share ('see', 'enter', vv. 3, 5) in the world to come, the eschatological realm. Jesus' response is that something radical and new is the prerequisite for seeing the

---

13. See Caragounis 2001:125, who also discusses other points which would indicate that the Fourth Gospel and the Synoptics 'share a common slate of traditions' (p. 126).

dominion of God (v. 3). There must be a second birth that is from above, which only God can effect. Men and women as such, even this Israelite, a senior religious leader, are not by nature able to attain this kingdom. Something radical, a complete renewal, with no connection with what has happened before, is a vital necessity.

This was not an acceptable response to a Pharisee, whose beliefs were that all Jews would enter the kingdom of God on the last day, with few exceptions.[14] But Jesus was saying that it is only those whom God 'makes new' who will 'see' (experience) the new age.[15] While this new age would almost automatically be thought of as coming in the future, in this Gospel it has come into existence in the present through the ministry and saving activity of Jesus the Messiah and Redeemer (cf. vv. 13–16); those who 'believe', whom God renews, experience it *now* (an emphasis in this Gospel) *as well as* in the future. Thus Jesus' stress is for the regeneration of an individual as a requirement before the end of the world, without which one would not be able even to enter the kingdom.

So for Jesus to talk to a Jew like Nicodemus, with his background and religious convictions, about seeing and entering the kingdom would have been interpreted as taking part in the kingdom at the end of the age, and participating in a resurrection life that was everlasting.

Possible reasons for use of 'kingdom of God' in John 3:3, 5

It is a reasonable question as to why 'kingdom of God' is used in John 3:3, 5, given its non-appearance elsewhere in this Gospel. It is hard to say for certain, but two suggestions are worth considering.

C. K. Barrett thinks that John was quite clear in his own mind that salvation had two key 'moments', which he spells out in the way he talks about eternal life as both present and future. On the

---

14. Those exceptions being those guilty of deliberate acts of apostasy and those who denied the faith – Mishnah *Sanhedrin* 10:1–4; noted by Kruse 2003:105 and Carson 1991:189.

15. It is interesting to note that in Matt. 19:28, the term 'kingdom' is replaced by *palingenesia*, 'renewal', 'regeneration', 'new birth', which is perhaps Matthew's equivalent for 'new age' (Beasley-Murray 1987:48).

one hand, a work has been completed, fulfilled in Christ, but on the other, there is a work to be yet consummated. So in this passage, he presented the language of Judaism ('kingdom of God') and the language of Hellenism ('to be born from above'), seeing this as an opportunity to set out what was neither really Jewish nor Hellenistic, but specifically Christian.[16] Usually, John was anxious to avoid a term that recalled apocalyptic Judaism, and Barrett suggests he uses it here to underline 'his criticism of a Judaism which was content to await the miraculous vindication of Israel in the kingdom of God and to ignore the necessity for inward conversion or rebirth'.[17]

On the other hand, it may simply be that John is using a traditional saying, indicating that he was aware that the Synoptics used such vocabulary to indicate the 'dynamic relationship humans can have with God'.[18] This earlier Christian tradition sometimes had Jesus speaking of the kingdom of God as a present reality,[19] but its image is predominantly eschatological. This future emphasis has been adapted by John to give his more realized understanding of Christian experience of eternal life.[20]

John 18:36

In chapter 18, Jesus is on trial and being questioned by Pilate, who asks if Jesus is the king of the Jews (v. 33). Pilate is concerned that Jesus, as a potential Jewish king, might be a threat to Rome and therefore to his position. In response, Jesus acknowledges that while he may not have soldiers to fight for him as earthly kings do, he is a king whose kingdom and authority are exercised

---

16. Barrett 1978:207.

17. Barrett 1978:207.

18. Borchert 1996:172.

19. See Matt. 5:10 ('Blessed are those who are persecuted for righteousness' sake, for theirs is the kingdom of heaven'); Mark 1:15 ('The time has come/is fulfilled,' Jesus said, 'The kingdom of God is/has come near/is at hand'); Luke 17:21 ('nor will they say, "Look, here it is!" or "There!" for behold, the kingdom of God is in the midst of you/within/among you').

20. See on this, Moloney 1998:93.

rather differently to any human authority. 'Kingship is the authority to lay down one's life as well as the authority to take it up again ... this is not the way human kings operate.'[21]

His 'reign', his 'kingship',[22] is not 'from this world'; its origin is not 'of this world' (which Barrett defines as 'the field in which humanity and the spiritual world are organized over against God'[23]); it is of a quite different order. Jesus' reign has a nature quite different to that of which Pilate has spoken.

Elsewhere in the Fourth Gospel, there are similar statements with terms like 'not from below', 'not of this world' (8:23; 17:16) or, positively, 'from heaven' or 'from above'. Jesus' kingship has an 'unworldly nature', but his 'sphere of operation' is in the world as eternal life is proclaimed.[24] Jesus is bringing salvation and judgment to humankind. Again, we note overlap with the ideas in the Synoptics, where the kingdom of God is not primarily of this age, but the age to come, although it is present in so far as through the ministry of Jesus that age has broken into this present age.[25] Jesus' kingship is 'the sovereign action of the Son through whom God performs his saving acts and speaks his saving words'.[26]

So 'Jesus does not deny that his kingdom or kingship affects the world, for the world will be conquered by those who believe in him (1 John 5:4). But he denies that his kingdom belongs to this world; like himself, it comes from above.'[27] And it is fair to say that as the Gospels show Jesus performing miracles among people, releasing them from Satan's rule and bringing God's blessing and his rule into their lives, they are thus describing the kingdom of God, his kingship in action in this world. This would seem to be what verses like Matthew 11:5 ('the blind receive their sight and

21. Leithart 2000:259.

22. Note the helpful comments on this by Beasley-Murray 1987:330.

23. Barrett 1978:536.

24. See Schnackenburg 1980:III, 249; Ridderbos 1997:593–595; Carson 1991:594.

25. Barrett 1978:536.

26. Beasley-Murray 1987:330.

27. Brown 1970:689.

the lame walk, lepers are cleansed and the deaf hear, and the dead are raised up, and the poor have good news preached to them') Matthew 12:28 ('But if it is by the Spirit of God that I cast out demons then the kingdom of God has come upon you'), as well as Matthew 13:16-17, Mark 4:11-12 (seen with what are known as the parables of the kingdom) and Luke 4:16-20 are indicating. And this fits in with the Johannine signs and their explanations.[28]

When one reads the Fourth Gospel, it sometimes seems there is a greater focus on a personal or internal view of the kingdom, so that a difference between the Synoptics and John is an external and corporate emphasis in the former, while the latter concentrates on a more subjective awareness of a person's position before God. Perhaps John 3:3, 5 does focus on an inner, new character that comes only from God. However, John 18:36 shows Jesus underlining the external importance and reality of the kingdom – 'My kingdom is not of this world . . .' (i.e. it is from another place). As Carl Henry summarizes, 'In John's gospel, as elsewhere, it is in Jesus that the kingdom impinges on and enters history, and through him participation is made available to humanity.'[29]

It is worth noting that the Fourth Gospel, perhaps more than the Synoptics, indicates very specifically the kingship of Jesus, a total of fourteen times.[30] Ten of the references refer to Jesus' trial before Pilate in chapters 18 and 19 (18:33, 37, 39; 19:3, 14, 15a, 19, 21). Indeed, the key theme of this trial is Jesus as king of the Jews. And this concerns what type of king Jesus actually is in contrast to what type of king Israel actually wants.

The trial (18:28 – 19:16) sees soldiers ridicule and beat Jesus at the

---

28. See on these points Beasley-Murray 1987:331.

29. Henry 1992:46.

30. E.g. John 1:49, 'You are the King of Israel', said Nathanael; 6:15 – the crowd after the feeding were about to come and make him king by force; 12:13 – at the triumphal entry, the crowd shouts, 'Blessed is he who comes in the name of the Lord, even the King of Israel!'; 12:15 – 'behold, your king is coming, sitting on a donkey's colt', as compared with Matthew (eight times), Mark (six times) and Luke (four times). This is noted by Caragounis 2001:125.

start of chapter 19. They seem to be performing a mock ceremony, making as if they are crowning him king of the Jews. A crown of thorns is thrust upon him, he is dressed in purple, and then presented to the crowds to be acclaimed as their king. He has an inscription above the cross that says he is king. But when Pilate presents Jesus to the crowd, instead of acclaiming him as their king, they cry out for his crucifixion. These Jews do not want Jesus as their king.

But of course, what is meant as mockery is actually true. Jesus *is* the king, and he says that just as he came into this world to testify to the truth, so anyone who wants to know the truth will recognize this (18:36–37). Pilate wants to acknowledge that Jesus is king when he puts the title above the cross not only in Hebrew but also in the major languages of the Gentiles (19:19, 20), despite the Jews' attempts to change what Pilate writes, which occurs only in John.

There is a good case for saying that it is not so much Jesus who is on trial here but the Jews (and Pilate!). They refuse to accept Jesus as their king, wanting to be like other nations – 'We have no king but Caesar' (19:15). On several occasions in this Gospel, the Jews have effectively put Jesus on trial, and now they think they have succeeded in having him condemned. But is this hour really one of judgment on Jesus? John is surely implying that it is they, the Jews, who are really on trial here, and they are judged and condemned. 'Israel as the people of Yahweh dies as soon as the leaders say, "We have no king but Caesar". Instead of bowing before the temple of God, the Jews have "destroyed this temple", the temple of Jesus' body. But he will rebuild it in three days.'[31] He is in charge, he is the King, the Lord. And for both John and the Synoptics, being a member of the kingdom of God means submitting to this lordship, recognizing Jesus as King. The trial narratives help to focus this.

Time of reception of the kingdom in John
In reflecting on the time of reception of the kingdom of God in John 3:3, 5, it is the view of C. C. Caragounis that these verses give no indication that this kingdom is to be thought of as 'a present

---

31. Leithart 2000:261, who also makes similar points on these verses (259–263).

reality'.[32] Jesus is talking here of how one may enter this kingdom; that is, what the conditions for entry are and the demands these place on an individual. There is no indication of the time this may take place. Similarly, Caragounis suggests that the reference to 'my kingdom' in 18:36 is to emphasize its other-worldly nature rather than to say it is currently present. This would seem to be the case in 18:36, but it is somewhat sweeping to say there is not any reference to receiving this kingdom in the present in John. The divine action enabling this birth from above to take place has a present referent (cf. also 3:15, 16, 18, 36). This will be considered further in the next chapter.

Possible reasons for lack of mention of the kingdom of God in the Fourth Gospel

While there seems to be some overlap and similarity of teaching on the kingdom between the Fourth Gospel and the Synoptics, it is nevertheless legitimate to ask why there is so little mention in the former of the 'kingdom of God' or 'kingdom'. A variety of explanations have been suggested, sometimes connected, with greater or lesser degrees of plausibility

John's previous conduct
An unlikely reason is noted by Leon Morris, who outlines the idea that the reason John omitted any emphasis on 'kingdom' is because he earlier completely misunderstood its nature and in fact tried to get the leading position in it (Mark 10:35–40). When he came to write the Fourth Gospel, he was thoroughly ashamed of such conduct and did not want to recall anything that reminded him of it.[33] This seems a speculative suggestion at best.

Enough said!
Similarly speculative is Guthrie's suggestion that in writing to sup-

---

32. Caragounis 1992a:475, n. 15; 2001:126–127.
33. See Morris 1995:190, n. 21.

plement the Synoptic Gospels, John was aware of how often 'kingdom of God' was mentioned, and so purposefully avoided such sayings, believing that there was no need to say any more on the subject.[34]

Encounters with Nicodemus and Pilate

It may be that the two mentions of 'the kingdom of God' in John 3:3, 5 and three mentions of 'kingdom' in John 18:36 simply reflect the actual meetings Jesus has with Nicodemus and Pilate and their specific thinking about, respectively, a Jewish kingdom and the Roman Empire. In the Fourth Gospel, it is clear that Jesus rejects any political ambitions.[35]

Avoidance of apocalyptic hope

A more likely suggestion is that John wished to avoid any connection with apocalyptic hope of the time, which focused on expectation of a Messiah who would vindicate Israel and bring in God's kingdom rule.[36] The resurrection era that Judaism awaited in the future had already been brought in with the resurrection of Christ.

Danger of misunderstanding

It is possible that John hesitated to use too much kingdom language because he was conscious of how it could be *misunderstood*. There are times when the term 'eternal life' stands in contrast to any misunderstanding of Jesus' kingdom in earthly/political terms. Thus, for example, as we have seen in John 3, Nicodemus thinks Jesus means *physical* birth (v. 5), while Jesus means spiritual birth bringing eternal life (vv. 3, 15, 16). Similarly, in chapter 4, the Samaritan woman wants/expects *physical* water, (vv. 9, 11 – 'Sir, . . . where do you get that living water? . . . give me this water, so that I will not be thirsty or have to come here to draw water', v. 15). But Jesus offers her living water (v. 13 – 'Everyone who drinks of this

---

34. Guthrie 1981:425.

35. On this see Köstenberger 2004:528.

36. See Caragounis 1992b:429.

water will be thirsty again . . . The water that I will give him will become in him a spring of water welling up to eternal life.' Compare 7:37–39, 'Out of his [the believer's] heart will flow rivers of living water'). Then in chapter 6, we see how the people want *physical* bread, but Jesus offers spiritual bread that leads to eternal life (v. 27). 'For the bread of God is he who comes down from heaven and gives life to the world' (v. 33). 'Whoever feeds on this bread will live for ever.' (See vv. 35, 51, 58.) Also in chapter 6, there were those who wanted to make Jesus a physical king by force (v. 15), while Pilate's concern was also that Jesus was an earthly king with an earthly kingdom (chs. 18, 19).[37]

To aid Hellenistic readers
L. Goppelt thinks that 'kingdom' was a typically Palestinian idea with Jewish national or apocalyptic connotations that primarily Hellenistic (Gentile) readers would struggle to understand, and so John substituted the term 'life', which Jesus had not used so much, but means something similar and was understood as a dynamic equivalent. We may compare Mark 9:43, 45 (= the kingdom in 9:47), 10:17 (cf. 10:15, 23), Matthew 25:46 (= the kingdom in v. 34) and Luke 10:25 for relevant points of comparison. This may be a reason for substituting 'life' for 'kingdom', but whether John's readership was predominantly Hellenistic rather than Jewish is doubtful.[38] 'Eternal life' has a Jewish background also,[39] so use of that term might not serve this purpose anyway.

Political ramifications
It could be that John avoided 'kingdom' language because it had political ramifications that might be harmful for believers living in Asia in the mid-nineties, given the imperial religious demands of the Roman state.[40]

---

37. For a stimulating discussion of misunderstandings in this Gospel see Carson 1982.
38. Goppelt 1982:45, cited by Keener 2003:328.
39. Keener 2003:328–329 and footnotes.
40. Keener 2003:328.

Emphasis on Christology

Caragounis suggests that John was writing to a church where the term 'kingdom of God' had been little used, as the person and work of Christ and teaching on the church had received greater stress.[41]

To emphasize personal salvation

Thompson argues that the term 'eternal life' emphasizes the more personal, individual aspects of salvation, its subjective experience, in ways more appropriate than 'kingdom of God'.[42]

Conclusions

So these various possibilities for the infrequent use of 'kingdom of God' have been suggested, and some are rather speculative. But in my view it is most likely that John was concerned to avoid misunderstanding in presenting his message and so used the term 'eternal life' to present a contrast with any understanding of a physical kingdom, which might have suggested a mistaken apocalyptic expectation.

It is worth making the point that even though the lexical count of the term 'kingdom (of God') is relatively rare in the Fourth Gospel, its meaning is present in other concepts, just as the term is not prominent in the Old Testament, but is nevertheless a central concept.[43] And so also for John this involved his presentation of eternal life. We should beware of drawing a contrast between the Fourth Gospel and the Synoptics on the basis of word count. As Caird helpfully summarizes:

> To see the Kingdom of God, to enter it, to be born of the Spirit, and to have eternal life are interchangeable descriptions of the one experience of salvation which is to become available to inquirers like Nicodemus only when Jesus has been 'lifted up', John 3:15. Jesus is indeed already King of Israel (1:50; 12:13, 15; cf. 20:31), but not in the only sense his enemies could understand. His sovereignty (18:36) is

---

41. Caragounis 1992b:429.

42. Thompson 1992:380.

43. See e.g. Carson 1991:188.

not derived from military strength and popular acclaim on which political power depends; it is derived from God who has entrusted to his Son the exercise of his own kingly authority.[44]

But let us now examine some examples of where the Synoptic Gospels use the term 'life' or 'eternal life' to see if that can help us to understand any connection in meaning between that and the kingdom of God.

'Eternal life' in the Synoptic Gospels

The Synoptic Gospels use the terms 'life' and 'eternal 'life' on a number of occasions (see e.g. Matt. 7:14; 19:16–17; Mark 9:43, 45, 47; 10:29–30; Luke 18:18, 24–26, 29–30). While these terms are used rather less than in the Fourth Gospel, it is interesting to note certain parallels and similarities in meaning.

Thus in *Mark 10:17–31* (and parallels in Matt. 19:16–30 and Luke 18:18–30), the rich young ruler asks Jesus what he must do to 'inherit eternal life' (v. 17). After Jesus tells him to keep the commandments, and then says that the key need is for him to sell his possessions and give the proceeds to the poor, he goes away shocked and sad. Jesus' comment to his disciples is that it is hard for those with wealth 'to enter the kingdom of God' (v. 23) and 'How difficult it is to enter the kingdom of God!' (v. 24). When the disciples respond with astonishment, 'Then who can be saved?', Jesus says that this is possible for nobody unless God intervenes and makes it possible (v. 27). He then goes on to say that there is no-one who has made sacrifices in terms of leaving houses or brothers, sisters, father or mother or children or fields or persecutions 'who will not receive a hundredfold now in this time . . . and in the age to come eternal life' (v. 30).

It would seem fair to say that these four phrases 'to inherit eternal life', 'to enter the kingdom of God', 'to be saved' and

---

44. Caird 1994:131–132 cited by Bock 2001:57, n. 1. This essay is posted on www.bible.org.

'eternal life in the age to come' are used with similar meanings, co-referentially. Salvation is a gift that God alone can give, and each term gives further understanding to the other.

We may also observe *Mark 9:43, 45, 47*, where Jesus speaks stern words about the sacrifices necessary in order to 'enter life' and avoid being thrown into *Gehenna* (vv. 43, 45). If one's hand is a problem, then it is better to cut it off in order to *enter life* maimed than to go to hell. Similar advice is given about a problem foot. And also an eye should be torn out if it is a cause of stumbling – 'It is better for you to *enter the kingdom of God* with one eye than with two eyes to be thrown into hell' (v. 47; my italics). It would seem that 'to enter life' and 'enter the kingdom of God' have similar referents. To enter life means to share in the life of the kingdom of God.

Similarly, *Mark 8:35* (parallels in Matt. 16:25 and Luke 9:24), (which talks about those who want to save their life will lose it, and those who lose their life for Christ's sake and the sake of the gospel, will save it) might be compared with John 12:25 – 'Whoever loves his life loses it, and whoever hates his life in this world will keep it for eternal life.' (We may note the use of *psychē* with reference to this earthly life in both verses.) John, as Mark, wants to contrast the 'life of this world', which can be lost, with the true, imperishable life not simply in terms of a 'temporal succession', but with reference to a more basic qualitative contrast. These points of contact would seem to indicate that at these stages at least, the Fourth Gospel and the Synoptics share a common tradition as well as similar theology.[45]

Matthew 25:34 and 46 also combine our two key phrases in a significant way in the parable of the sheep and the goats. The king says to those at his right hand, 'Come, you who are blessed by my Father, *inherit the kingdom* prepared for you from the foundation of the world . . .' (v. 34, my italics), and concludes concerning those at his left and right hands, 'And these will go away into eternal punishment, but the righteous into *eternal life*' (v. 46, my italics). Thus

---

45. As Schnackenburg puts it, 'it is beyond dispute that a synoptic saying is here (John 12:25) being used and reformulated' (1980: II, 353).

inheriting the kingdom seems to be presented in a similar way to entering into eternal life.

It is fair to conclude that the terms 'eternal life' and 'the kingdom of God' are used in these passages in ways that suggest strongly they are co-referential terms. It is further fair to say the orientation of eternal life in the Synoptics is more to the future. 'Eternal life is the prize of salvation, the essence of what is expected from the kingdom of God.'[46]

But if these verses seem to give us grounds for seeing close connection in terms of understanding eternal life and the kingdom of God as being consistent in their meaning, there are perhaps even clearer parallels with John 3:3, 5.

Matthew 18:3	Mark 10:15	John 3:3, 5
and said, 'Truly, I say to you, unless you turn and become like children, you will never enter the kingdom of heaven.'	Truly, I say to you, whoever does not receive the kingdom of God like a child shall not enter it.	Jesus answered him, 'Truly, truly, I say to you, unless one is born again he cannot see the kingdom of God.' . . . Jesus answered, 'Truly, truly, I say to you, unless one is born of water and the Spirit, he cannot enter the kingdom of God.'

It is often suggested that a clear parallel to what is said in John 3:3, 5 is to be found in Matt. 18:3 and maybe Mark 10:15 (parallel Luke 18:17). Thus Caragounis comments, 'These two sayings (Mark 10:15 and Matt. 18:3), which bring together the ideas of conversion and receiving the kingdom of God as a child, are the closest ideological parallels to John 3:3, 5, which speaks of

---

46. Schnackenburg 1980: II, 353.

"being born again" ("from above", *anōthen*) as a condition for entering the kingdom.'[47] Two articles make particular comments on this. One, by Barnabas Lindars,[48] seeks to demonstrate that John is dependent on a tradition behind Matthew (both of which go back to a common Aramaic original), except that John has *gennēthē anōthen* (born from above) for *straphēte kai genēsthe hōs ta paidia* (turn/ change/be converted and become as children). 'To "become as children" does not mean to become childlike, but to become comparable to children, i.e. in the same situation as children.'[49] Lindars thinks this means a spiritual regeneration, the source of which is to be found in God. It is a call for a radical renewal in order to be ready for the coming kingdom. He thus sees clear similarities in what is presented in John 3:3, 5 and Matthew 18:3.

The second article is by John Pryor[50] and his main contention is that in John 3:3, 5, we have 'a deliberate and conscious commentary on a tradition known to the Johannine community, which was similar to that reflected in Matt. 18:3'.[51] The teaching in the Matthean saying is closer to John 3:3, 5 than that in Mark 10:15.

Both writers are agreed that there is a Johannine dependence on a common tradition behind John 3:3, 5,[52] although they argue their cases in different ways and, at points, Pryor is critical of

---

47. Caragounis 2001:127.

48. Lindars 1980–1:287–294.

49. Lindars 1980–1:290.

50. Pryor 1991.

51. Pryor 1991:71.

52. It is interesting to note the comment made by Dunn when he considers these verses in Matt. 18:3, Mark 10:15, Luke 18:17 in connection with Jesus' words in John 3:3, 5: he considers that the challenge to Nicodemus is 'closely paralleled' in the Synoptic verses, and that 'John 3 seems to be an elaboration of that basic claim made by Jesus' (1985:38). See also Witherington 1992:64, 266, n. 21, where he suggests that John 3:5 'seems to be conveying the same sort of idea as we find in the synoptic saying, and may indeed be an alternative form of that saying'. See also Keener 2003:I, 544, n. 116.

Lindars.[53] While Köstenberger is critical of their arguments[54] concerning John's dependence on the tradition behind Matthew 18:3, it is nonetheless useful to see how they discuss the teaching in these verses.

When Mark says that it is necessary to receive the kingdom like a little child (Mark 10:15), it would seem that a person must have an 'attitude of open-handed childlike helplessness that receives the grace of God as pure gift'.[55] There must be a 'childlike acceptance' of both the gift that comes from God as well as the demands the kingdom places upon one (cf. Mark 9:33–37, where humility and concern for others are presented as necessary in order truly to serve God). A child has no rights or status, no grounds to claim a place in the kingdom, which must therefore be received solely as a gift.

Matthew 18:3 seems to have a slightly different emphasis. It underlines the need for repentance and childlike helplessness, openness, acceptance and simplicity in order to enter the kingdom.[56] But Matthew then goes on (v. 4) to emphasize humility before God, an acknowledgment of childlike dependence on him ('Whoever humbles himself like this child is the greatest in the kingdom of heaven'). The fact that repentance is required would seem to indicate that there is also a need to change one's way of life. So 'moral change and newness of life' are involved in 'becoming as a child', even the need in effect 'to become a new being', a radical requirement.[57]

This has close affinities with what John 3:3, 5 is saying. Here there is a 'call for new being, a new being so totally new that it bears no relationship to one's natural existence (v. 6) and which is effected by

53. See Pryor 1991:80f., 87.

54. Köstenberger 2004:122, n. 21 – 'unpersuasive and unnecessary'.

55. Pryor 1991:92 and references in n. 1 on that page.

56. Compare Caragounis 2001:127: 'The Synoptic sayings are constructed around the motif of the child as a natural representative of the qualities necessary for inheriting the kingdom of God (openness, simple trust and acceptance).'

57. Pryor 1991:92f.

God himself . . .'[58] 'It could not have been expressed more radically.'[59]

We conclude that there is a considerable degree of overlap in the teaching of these sayings, and whatever one concludes about their precise relationship in terms of literary connections, the closeness of their teaching is another indication of the integral relationship of the Fourth Gospel with the Synoptics. Thus C. K. Barrett considers that Jesus' response to Nicodemus and the whole notion of 'supernatural begetting' has no direct parallel with the Old Testament or Judaism, and this is not accidental,

since the point of this paragraph is to bring out the fact that the Old

---

58. Pryor 1991:93.

59. Caragounis 2001:127. Some think that to modify 'becoming (once more) as children' into 'becoming a child' understood as new creation, birth from above, is too great a step in understanding: 'the *hōs* [as] is an essential element of both forms of the Synoptic logion, just as on the other hand the Johannine logion is not concerned with man's conversion, but with God's action upon man' (Schnackenburg 1980:I, 367, cited by Pryor 1991:73). However, this change (from 'becoming as' to becoming a child) is not so great, especially if one interprets the former as indicating a need for 'radical renewal', an openness to change and a humility and dependence on God to act (Lindars 1980–1:290 and n. 7). Furthermore, Pryor points out that to say that Matthew and Mark emphasize human conversion while John emphasizes God's action is not such a great contrast. If one understands 'receive the kingdom like a child' as underlining a willingness and openness to receive this gift of God, rather than any notion of human achievement or merit, then the closeness between the verses is apparent. Surely highlighted here is humanity in its need of God's help and grace (Pryor 1991:73).

Also, 'in the Great Thanksgiving [Matt. 11:25], the *nēpioi* ("infants", "little children") are those to whom the revelation is given by the Father and the Son. So the demand to become as children is balanced by the recognition that the grace of revelation is given to such' (Pryor 1991:73–74). And it is certainly fair to say that in Jesus' conversation with Nicodemus, he is giving such a challenge to this Pharisee and making demands of him to which Nicodemus needs to respond.

Testament religion and Judaism, which Nicodemus, the Pharisee and
ruler of the Jews, the teacher of Israel, represents, is inadequate; it
cannot move forward continuously into the kingdom of God. A
moment of discontinuity, comparable with physical birth, is essential.

Barrett then goes on to say that the source of this new terminology is essentially and primarily 'the primitive gospel tradition'
such as that found in Matthew 18:3 (cf. Mark 10:15; Luke 18:17).
And from these sayings are derived the New Testament teachings
about not merely expecting the kingdom of God in the future (the
age to come), but to perceive it already ('germinally or potentially')
in the coming of Jesus.[60]

Concluding summary

We have noted a number of differences between the Synoptic
Gospels and the Fourth Gospel. Some of these are more
significant than others, and in any case none is insurmountable
as far as the reliability of the Fourth Gospel is concerned.[61]
Concerning the usage of eternal life and kingdom (of God), it
would seem that there is considerable overlap in their meaning.
There may well be an underlying common tradition between the
Synoptics and John,[62] and while the term 'kingdom of God' is
used infrequently in the latter, it is possible to suggest reasons for
this.[63] Similarly, we can posit arguments for its adoption in John
3:3, 5,[64] where John is adapting what is normally a future usage to

---

60. Barrett 1978:206–207. See also Saunders and Mastin 1968:123–124;
    Keener 2003:544. G. E. Ladd comments that in Mark 10:15, the kingdom
    of God is a reality to be received in the present in order to enter it in the
    future. 'Present and future are inseparably bound together. There is no
    reason not to understand the Johannine saying in the same way' (1975:303).
61. See on this the bibliographic references on p. 56, n. 5.
62. Noted on p. 60 above.
63. See pp. 66–70 above.
64. See pp. 61–62 above.

underline his desire to indicate a realized experience of eternal life.

Jesus' conversation with Pilate in John 18 underlines his unique authority as well as the nature of his kingship and kingdom, which are in sharp contrast to this world. Again, overlap with the Synoptics' description of these matters may be noted.[65] Both the external and internal nature of God's kingdom are apparent in the four Gospels. Jesus as king is a particular emphasis of the Fourth Gospel, but the need to submit to his lordship is clear in each Gospel.

Examination of the occurrences of 'eternal life' in the Synoptic Gospels indicated connections and consistency in meaning with 'kingdom of God', and the close relationship between the Fourth Gospel and the Synoptics was again underlined.[66] Particularly noteworthy was the connection in meaning and close theological parallels between John 3:3, 5 and Matthew 18:3 and Mark 10:15.

Thus while there might at first sight appear to be a contrast between the two terms, a careful examination reveals evidence for a close connection between what it means to be a member of the kingdom of God and to have eternal life. These may be seen as co-referential terms, as various scholars underline:

Eternal life and the kingdom of God are closely allied concepts for John.[67]

The two (eternal life and Kingdom of God) are dynamic equivalents for the believers' eschatological experience of divine salvation.[68]

---

65. See pp. 63–64 above.

66. See pp. 70–76 above.

67. Brown 1970:I, 159.

68. Caragounis 1992a:474. Also 'In my view, the Johannine talk of "eternal life" is equivalent to the synoptic habit of speaking of the Kingdom of God, with the proviso that these are different concepts, in an analogous way as when Paul speaks of "justification by faith" or Peter of "conversion" or John of "being born again" — even though each one them describes salvation from a different point of view, each with its own particular nuances and emphases' (C. C. Caragounis, email correspondence, February 2005).

> Life and eternal life are used interchangeably, and can also be used in place of 'kingdom of God' to speak of the state of blessedness that one participates in through faith in Jesus.[69]

> John 'has specifically set out teaching which stresses eternal life in a manner parallel to the synoptic kingdom teaching'.[70]

Some comments from G. E. Ladd may help to summarize key points. It is interesting to note that in the Fourth Gospel, eternal life is first mentioned after the only references it contains to the kingdom of God (3:3, 5, 15). If eternal life may be defined broadly as the life of the age to come, in the Synoptics, this is also life in the kingdom of God, which belongs to the age to come. But in the Synoptics, that future kingdom has broken into this present age – Matthew 12:28 – although there is still a future age to come. In the Fourth Gospel, a similar idea is present. 'In this, "eternal life" in John resembles the kingdom of God in the synoptic Gospels. That which is properly a future blessing becomes a present fact in virtue of the future in Christ.'[71] So while these are different idioms, and they are not entirely identical, 'the underlying theological structure is the same, although expressed in different categories. If eternal life is indeed the life of the eschatological kingdom of God, and if the kingdom is present, it follows that we might expect the Kingdom to bring . . . a foretaste of the life of the future age'.[72]

© Paul Woodbridge, 2006.

---

69. Thompson 1992:380.
70. Guthrie 1981:425.
71. Barrett 1978:215, cited by Ladd 1975:259.
72. Ladd 1975:259.

3. THEOLOGICAL IMPLICATIONS OF 'ETERNAL LIFE' IN THE FOURTH GOSPEL

Paul Woodbridge

Having established the close relationship between the terms 'kingdom of God' and 'eternal life' in the Synoptics and the Fourth Gospel, we can now consider various uses and theological implications of John's use of the term 'eternal life', as well as possible practical implications.

Meaning of 'eternal life' in the Fourth Gospel

If it is reasonable to say that 'eternal life' and 'kingdom of God' are co-referential terms, what more precisely does John mean by the term *eternal life*?

It is clear that John's aim in writing his Gospel is that 'you may believe that Jesus is the Christ, the Son of God, and that *by believing you may have life in his name*' (20:31, my italics). Jesus' aim may be summarized as 'that they may have *life and have it abundantly*' (10:10,

---

1. 3:15, 16, 36; 4:14, 36; 5:24, 39; 6:27, 40, 54, 68; 10:28; 12:25, 50; 17:2, 3.

my italics). The term 'eternal life' occurs sixteen times in the Fourth Gospel[1] while the word 'life' occurs thirty-two times.[2] A number of these latter references appear to use 'life' interchangeably with 'eternal life' (e.g. 3:36: 'Whoever believes in the Son has eternal life; whoever does not obey the Son shall not see life, but the wrath of God remains on him'; and see also 5:24, 29, 40).

Jewish background

The phrase 'eternal life' appears in the Septuagint only in Daniel 12:2, where it translates 'the life of the age' (Hebrew *ḥayyê 'ôlām*),[3] indicating the life inherited in the future at the resurrection of the dead – the righteous are raised up to 'everlasting life'. While 'life' in the Old Testament tended to focus on a positive earthly existence seen as a gift from God and enjoyed in relationship with him (see e.g. Deut. 30:15–20), rather than any notion of immortality, gradually the thought that even death could not damage this relationship emerged and death would be transcended (see hints of this in Pss. 16:9–11 and 49:15). This then led to an assurance of a resurrection body and life in the coming age (see Dan. 12:1–2).

'The life of the world to come' or 'life of the age' ('eternal life') occur quite frequently in Jewish sources, with the thought that the righteous are kept safe for life in the coming world after death (cf. *Psalms of Solomon* 3:12; 13:11; 14:10; *1 Enoch* 37:4; 58:3). There is

---

2. 1:4; 3:36; 5:21, 24, 26, 29, 40; 6:33, 35, 48, 51, 53, 63; 7:1; 8:11, 12; 9:3; 10:10, 11, 15, 17; 11:25, 53; 12:25; 13:37, 38; 14:6; 15:13; 20:31.

3. This Hebrew form occurs only here in the Old Testament, although it is taken up in later Jewish literature. It is usually agreed that Dan. 12:1–2 is the only passage that specifically affirms belief in the resurrection of the dead in the Hebrew Bible. Other verses seem to indicate a move towards belief in some kind of existence after death (such as Ps. 16:11; Isa. 26:19; 53:10–12) and may contribute to the resurrection belief in Dan. 12. Those who favour a second-century date for Daniel would argue that the use of this term *ḥayyê 'ôlām*, which occurs in intertestamental literature, is evidence for a later date than the traditional sixth century. For further discussion see Collins 1993:394–398 ('Excursus: On Resurrection'); Lucas 2002:294–296, 301–305; Wright 2003:109–115.

also a contrast of 'this age' and 'the Age to Come' found in a book such as *4 Ezra*, although not the term 'eternal life', and it would be fair to say that eternal life in Judaism, as in Daniel 12:2, focuses mainly on the life of the Age to Come, resurrection life.[4]

Johannine teaching

We have seen in the previous chapter that while the Synoptics also speak of 'eternal life', their greater focus in doing so is on the life of the future age (e.g. Matt. 25:46; Mark 10:17, 21, 23, 30). In John, this *future thrust* is retained in many places. Thus when Jesus says in John 3:36, 'whoever does not obey the Son shall not see life', he is referring to a person's ultimate destiny, one of condemnation (cf. 3:18). This future, eschatological character is also clearly seen in John 12:25, where persons who hate their life 'in this world' will keep it 'for eternal life'. (This verse is strongly reminiscent of Matt. 10:39; Mark 8:35; and Luke 9:24.) The person who drinks of the living water, of the Spirit who alone gives life, this water will be a source of life in the age to come (John 4:14). Those to whom Jesus has given eternal life he will raise up at the last day – John 6:40b, 54. Those who eat the bread Jesus gives, which came down from heaven, will live for ever (John 6:51, 58). Those who believe in Jesus, even though they experience physical death, will live (11:24, 25). At the end, Jesus will return and take his own to himself (14:3: 'And if I go and prepare a place for you, I will come again and will take you to myself, that where I am you may be also'). This eternal life is to be experienced at the last day when the righteous will rise 'to the resurrection of life', and the wicked 'to the resurrection of condemnation' (5:28–29).

But noteworthy in John is an emphasis on the *present state of salvation*. John 1:18 indicates that Jesus Christ has made God known, and that this was a key reason for his coming to earth. From the believer's point of view, experience of eternal life takes place in the present, as well as existing in the future. Thus 3:18

4. For more detail on the Jewish background see Dalman 1909:156–158; Dodd 1953:144–146; Ladd 1975:255–256; Schnackenburg 1980:II, 356–360; Keener 2003:I, 328–329.

(no condemnation for those who believe), belief produces eternal life now, and no judgment at all (5:24; 6:40a [note present tenses adjacent to a future: 'everyone who looks on the Son and believes in him should have eternal life, and I will raise him up on the last day']; and 6:47). Thus the life of the age to come has, to some extent at least, already been imparted to the believer. Jesus came to give people a present experience of the future life (10:10). This experience of life is a gift to believers who thus belong to Christ in the present as they hear his voice and follow him (10:27). This gift is irrevocable – those who receive it will never ever perish and no-one can take away this life (10:28 – note the strength of the negatives in this verse). This reception takes place in the present. Another reason for believers' eternal security is that the Father, who has given these people to his Son, is greater than all and there is no chance at all that anyone or anything can snatch these sheep from the Father's hand (10:29). The unity of the Father and Son is a further reason for such security (10:30). We might say that since this eternal life is a present experience, eternity has broken into time, and may be experienced now, before death.

Christ came from heaven to give life to the world (6:33), to resolve the hunger and thirst of whoever comes to him as the Bread of Life (6:35). Indeed, his very words are life (6:63), because they come from the Father who has given him commandment about what to say, and this commandment is eternal life (12:49–50). And this life not only comes through Jesus and his words; it is contained in his very person (5:26: 'For as the Father has life in himself, so he has granted the Son also to have life in himself'). He himself is the living bread who gives life (6:51ff.), as well as the living water (4:10, 14). Jesus claims also to be the life (11:25; 14:6), for God as its ultimate source has granted the Son to have life in himself (5:26). As the Son depends on the Father, so also believers have life inasmuch as they also depend on the Father through the mediating work of the Son.[5]

---

5. The relations of these matters to the death of Christ will be considered under the heading 'Divine necessity' below (pp. 91–94).

In many ways, 17:3 is an appropriate summary: 'This is eternal life, that they know you the only true God, and Jesus Christ whom you have sent.' So knowing God *is* eternal life – ongoing, incorruptible fellowship with God which can never be ended, not even by physical death. This is a strong, personal, even intimate, knowledge and relationship with God. Perhaps we may connect it with John 14:23: ' If anyone loves me, he will keep my word, and my Father will love him, and we will come to him and make our home with him.' So eternal life for John is having a loving relationship of fellowship with both God the Father and with his Son Jesus Christ through his Spirit, which commences here in the present and goes on after death.[6] We enjoy in the present eschatological blessings which will come to fulfilment and completion when Jesus returns. He is present now through his Spirit (thus 14:16–18, 23), but will return to take his followers to a place he has prepared for them (14:2, 3). It is the Spirit who gives life, eternal life, and John 7:39 indicates that this Spirit is sent by the crucified, risen and exalted Jesus to those who believe. It is his ministry to present the life of the kingdom of God to men and women, to grant them rebirth (John 3:3, 5, 6). This is shown also in John 4:10, 13, 14, where Jesus indicates that the 'gift of God', the water he gives, is the life that is granted by the Spirit. This water is 'an assurance of life for the believer from the Spirit who ever remains to bind him to the Lord of life'.[7]

Conclusions

A consideration of these verses has shown that there is both a future and a present emphasis in the John's Gospel, with a noteworthy stress on the latter that is not found in the Synoptics. Yet these two dimensions of life are closely connected in Jesus'

---

6. For details on eternal life and eschatology in the Fourth Gospel see especially Ladd 1975:256–269 and 298–308; Carson 1981:134–146; Beasley-Murray 1987:lxxv–lxxxvii; Morris 1989:143–144, 195–196, 204–205; Carson 1991:97–98; Smalley:1998:265–270; Keener 2003:I, 320–323, 328–329.

7. Beasley-Murray 1991:69, who outlines similar points on 68f. See also Ladd 1975:288–290; Guthrie 1981:527–529.

discourse about his relationship with the Father. Since the Father is the source of life, it is only he who can raise the dead; but he has given and trusted this prerogative to his Son (5:21). And it seems this mission of raising the dead has a two-stage fulfilment: According to 5:25, the time ('hour') has already come when the dead hear the Son of God's voice and come to life. It seems fair to say that this refers to a 'spiritual' resurrection (i.e. a present experience of eternal life), given the words 'the hour is coming *and is now here*'. So this event of rising into life is taking place in Jesus' ministry, and a key reason for this is that the Father has granted his Son to have life in himself (5:26). But this present experience is not all there is, since the time is coming when those who are physically dead ('in the tombs') will hear Jesus' voice and come out (5:28).[8] Thus we have an emphasis on the 'dynamic presence' of eternal life in the words and mission of Jesus, and the eventual full realization of God's rule to take place in the future, a Johannine tension that is present in other parts of the New Testament. One may draw a parallel with what the Synoptics say about the kingdom of God being present as a 'dynamic entity' and also still to be fully realized.[9]

Challenge to futurist emphasis: R. Bultmann

While this evidence seems to indicate that John places together these present and future aspects of eschatology in creative tension and in a close bond, a number of writers have found this juxtaposition hard to accept.[10] Perhaps best known is Rudolf Bultmann,

---

8. See on this Ladd 1975:258; Wenham 1997:16–17; Johnson 1992: 469–471. Keener notes that it is likely that both realized and future eschatology 'coexisted in the Qumran community without conscious tension. The same could have been true of the Johannine community' (Keener 2003:I, 322).

9. See on these points and other relevant comments, de Jonge 1992:481 and *passim*.

10. For a convenient and succinct discussion of ways of understanding the relationship of present and future eschatologies in this Gospel see Kysar:1975:209–214.

followed similarly by a number of others. His view was that John's effort to relate future, eschatological hope to the present saving action of Christ meant that he 'demythologized' eschatology. Thus on 12:31, he says:

> The judgment of this world now takes place. The ruler of this world will
> now be thrown out of the domain over which he formerly held sway . . .
> the Evangelist's language . . . serves to eliminate the traditional
> eschatology of primitive Christianity. The turn of the ages results now
> . . . the destiny of man has become definitive according as each grasps
> the meaning of this 'now', according as he believes or not. No future in
> this world's history can bring anything new, and all apocalyptic pictures
> of the future are empty dreams.[11]

According to Bultmann, any references in this Gospel to resurrection and judgment 'on the last day' are due to a later editor, an 'ecclesiastical redactor', who changed the text in an effort to bring its overall message into line with the church generally. This person is responsible for such texts as 5:28, 29; 6:39, 40, 44, 54; 12:48.[12] But this sort of view hardly does justice to the evidence of the Gospel as a whole.[13] Beasley-Murray makes some important summarizing points in this regard.[14] John's concerns focus not only on the consequences in the present of the work of the incarnate Christ, not only on that risen Christ's present activity, but also on 'the presentation of the risen Lord that extends to the future horizons, as 5:17 intimates'. If one considers 11:25, this verse covers both a future and a present resurrection – 'Christ as the Resurrection gives hope for the future life, and the reality of that life is the present.' John 3:16–21 implies the same about judgment – verse 16 indicates a future judgment, while verses 18–21 talk of a process of judgment which will be revealed at the last day (v. 21; note also 12:31–32 and 47 for juxtaposition of present and future).

---

11. Bultmann 1971:431.
12. Bultmann 1971:11, 236, 259, 261–262.
13. See also the critical comments of de Jonge 1992:482.
14. Beasley-Murray 1987:lxxxvi–lxxxvii.

The parousia also is talked about in the future in 14:3, but anticipated in the present in 14:23.[15]

Yet some writers attempt to affirm that John retains early
eschatological traditions, while judging that these are actually
inconsistent with his real emphasis on a present experience of
eternal life which the incarnate Jesus has brought, and so the
former have lost any real relevance for him. Others argue that
John keeps a future emphasis because he thinks that these elements have not been completely fulfilled in Christ's earthly ministry.
It is not easy to bring these two modes of thinking together, and
one wonders whether either approach really does justice to this
Gospel's material.

Realized emphasis

It is fair to say that the Fourth Gospel lays greater stress on a realized eschatology than the Synoptics. One reason sometimes given
for this is the so-called 'delay' of the parousia. Expectation of its
imminence faded as time went on, and so John focused more on
the present ministry of Christ in the believer through the Holy
Spirit and the experience of eternal life *now*. However, it is doubtful that this 'problem' was such a serious matter for the early
church, and in any case it is possible to argue that John's emphasis
is due more specifically to his own understanding of and desire to
interpret accurately the actual teaching of Jesus. Thus C. H. Dodd
thinks that the Fourth Gospel contains a careful exposition of
Jesus' teaching,[16] and others have concurred.

---

15. See also the helpful comments in Beasley-Murray 1991:5–7.
16. Dodd 1936:75. Burge notes that while hope of the parousia was not lost,
    the coming of the Paraclete helped to underline the present hope
    (1987:34). Similarly, Schnackenburg denies that there was a problem
    arising out of a 'delay of the Parousia' in the fourth Gospel (1980:II, 436).
    Smalley 1998:166–168 also argues against the parousia's delay being
    significant for John. He also considers the issue of the delay in a similar
    vein in the Synoptics and Paul in *JBL* 83 (1964):41–54. Bauckham

Another reason for this realized emphasis is that while both Pharisees and Christians shared a future perspective, it was more important for John to lay emphasis on a realized approach in a Gospel written partly to deal with Jewish opponents who acknowledged a future hope but who denied that it was Jesus Christ who had inaugurated that hope.[17]

Challenge to realized emphasis: C. C. Caragounis

A different approach to this matter is taken by Chrys Caragounis. He argues strongly that it is mistaken to understand any of John's supposedly 'realized' teachings in that way. In two extremely stimulating articles,[18] he examines some key texts which are often put forward in support of a realized eschatology and suggests what he thinks is a more accurate way of understanding them.

In his first article (1992a), he asks how solid the basis is for claiming that 'the eschatological reign of God over men was thought either by Jesus himself or by the Early Church, to have been initiated in any real sense already during the ministry of Jesus and to be evidenced by his miracles?'[19] In particular, concerning the Fourth Gospel, he argues that verses often put forward to support a realized eschatology[20] because of their use of the present tense (e.g. 3:36: the one who 'believes in the Son *has* eternal life') could equally be interpreted as indicating that those who believe receive eternal life 'at some future point of time (i.e. at the resurrection)'.[21] Faith is a condition for receiving this life, and these verses thus explain the *means* by which eternal life is acquired, not the present receiving of it. Eternal life is in

---

(1980:3–36) looks at eschatological delay in Jewish apocalyptic, general rabbinic debate in the late first century AD, the Apocalypse of Baruch, 2 Peter 3 and the Apocalypse of John.

17. See Keener 2003:323. He cites Brown 1982:99 on this point.
18. Caragounis 1992a:473-480; 2001:125–134.
19. Caragounis 1992a:475.
20. Such as 3:36; 5:24; 6:47; and 6:54.
21. Caragounis 1992a:476. See also 2001:131.

fact still future from the standpoint of these sayings. The whole thrust of John, he argues, is to emphasize eternal life being available to anyone who believes in Jesus without any reference to time at all.

Furthermore, verses such as 12:23 ('The hour has come for the Son of Man to be glorified'), 13:31 ('Now is the Son of Man glorified') and 17:4 ('I glorified you on earth') all use what Caragounis calls an idiomatic past tense, 'which transports an event from the future to the present in order to enhance its reality and force by underlying its certainty and especially its imminence'.[22] Similarly, a verse such as 3:18 referring to the fact that a person who believes 'is not condemned' (present tense) actually indicates a future significance in that it reveals that a believer's faith has ensured no final judgment. Similarly, an unbeliever is condemned (present tense) because of unbelief, although this judgment is clearly a future event. The verdict is already settled because of either belief or unbelief. The same principle is also apparent in 5:24: 'the properly future, eschatological passing from death to life is described as if it were an already accomplished event in view of the fact that the decisive action for it – faith in Jesus – has already taken place'.[23]

This line of argument, Caragounis suggests, indicates not only that the specific actions are future from the speaker's standpoint, but also rule out their interpretation in terms of realized eschatology. A similar principle may be seen, he argues, in the texts that talk about Jesus' time or 'hour' as 'having come' (12:23; 17:1). This does not mean the time of his death had arrived, but that it was very close – the past tense indicates a future albeit imminent event. Jesus 'is on his way to Gethsemane and his work can therefore be viewed as though it were already accomplished'.[24] A final example may be seen in 5:25 ('Truly, truly, I say to you, an hour is coming, and is now here, when the dead will hear the voice of the Son of God, and those who hear will live'). Caragounis does not think this supports a realized interpretation, but rather suggests a future completion of an event. The saying 'has not acquired the status of realization . . . "now is" only emphasizes the

---

22. Caragounis 2001:131.

23. Caragounis 1992a:479.

24. Caragounis 1992a:479.

imminence of the "coming" '. Jesus is actually 'speaking of the time following his death, an event that has not yet taken place'.[25]

In conclusion, Caragounis suggests that the eschatology of John's Gospel, as in the Synoptics, 'has a future orientation', even if this future 'is decided in the present'. A decision in the present on whether one will believe or not in Jesus dictates a person's future once and for all. Thus 'present faith is transmuted into eternal life while unbelief is transmuted into condemnation'. At another level, it may also have been that John 'allowed the post-resurrection time perspective to influence his expression speaking of events that in the former *Sitz im Leben* were future, but now had been realized'. This is different from realized eschatology, which implies that various eschatological events have already taken place during the life of Jesus. For Caragounis,

> the Eschaton, eternal life, and judgment, which are essentially future events, are potentially 'present' in Jesus during his ministry, since they are bound up with his destiny, and they are spoken of as 'present' realities only in principle inasmuch as the predetermined hour of Jesus, which is to actually initiate them, is irrevocable and imminent.

Thus we should think of John's eschatology not as 'realized', but as 'potential', a 'potentially present eschatology'.[26]

There is much that is helpful and stimulating in what Caragounis says. Perhaps some have placed too much emphasis on a 'realized' eschatology, and been in danger of underplaying the future empha-sis that is clearly taught in this Gospel. It is also true that people's decision whether to believe or not dictates their destiny. Similarly, it is valuable to note that Jesus' 'hour', his time of glorification, is future from the point of view of the Fourth Gospel's literary setting. Yet it is surely hard to avoid an understanding of this

---

25. Caragounis 2001:132. John 7:37–39 and 11:51–52 illustrate the same principle – see 1992a:480, n. 37.

26. The quotes and details of this paragraph come from Caragounis 1992a:480; 2001:134. For technical evidence in support of this position see Caragounis 2004:261–278.

Gospel's eschatology that indicates a present experience of salvation, a receiving of eternal life *as soon as one believes*, and its both objective and subjective reality at the time, so to speak, even while allowing for its future completion and fulfilment. In an email, I asked Caragounis how he would fit John 17:3 into his pattern of a potential eschatology rather than a realized experience of knowing God in the present. His response was:

> You are quite right to say that John 17:3 represents a process that has already begun, that is, that the disciples have already begun 'knowing' Jesus. But this process is not finished. Thus, in vv. 25–26 he can say 'they have known . . . I have made known to them' and at the same time 'I will make known'. So, too, John 16:13 'The Parakletos will guide you into all truth'. The synoptic Kingdom of God functions in an analogous way. Even though it is primarily a future concept, in the sense of their entering into it, the decision takes place now and depends on their attitude of faith or lack of faith to Jesus.[27]

I would certainly not want to say that the process has finished. However, this does not seem to negate understanding the verses cited on pages 81–84 above (in favour of a realized eschatology) as losing their present thrust. John (Jesus) communicates a present experience of eternal life as well as underlining its future fulfilment and culmination, and these things complete and confirm each other.[28] Salvation 'now is' as well as 'is coming'.

The significance of the exaltation of the glorified Jesus

A key emphasis of the Fourth Gospel is that eternal life is available to anyone who believes in the present, with a future

---

27. Email communication, 12 February 2005. Caragounis also indicated a number of unfortunate errors in the text of his 2001 article, due mainly to his original article being shortened without his knowledge!

28. See also some useful comments on these matters by de Jonge 1992:481–487; and Scholtissek 2004:466–468.

consummation eventually to take place. John 6:54 and 11:25, 26 are key verses for bringing these aspects of John's eschatology together. This has been called an *inaugurated* eschatology[29] – by Christ's coming, death, resurrection and ascension, eternal life is made available in the present, and in looking to his return, we consider the exalted and glorified Christ who dispenses many benefits of eternal life to people who believe now. He is the king, the one who rules and grants eternal life. Some ways in which this is drawn out by John will now be considered.

Divine necessity

A basic conviction of the Fourth Gospel is the divine necessity of the death of Christ. This is portrayed in a number of ways, not least by the word *dei* ('it is necessary' or this *must* happen): thus 3:14 – the Son of Man *must* be lifted up (also 12:34); also Jesus lays down his life as a command of his Father (10:17–18 and 14:31); he is 'lifted up' so that the purpose of his coming might be achieved in drawing all people to himself (12:24, 32). As far as understanding the concept of Jesus' glorification is concerned, his crucifixion is an essential element of this, as may be seen in the references to Jesus' 'hour' (12:23; 13:31–32; 17:1).

If we were to ask the purpose of Christ's death, then a number of verses need to be considered. First, the witness of John the Baptist in John 1:29, 36 – 'the Lamb of God, who takes away the sin of the world.' A number of options are put forward as to the precise significance of this phrase,[30] but it is fair to say that John is pointing to Jesus as the one who will bring about the reconciliation of the world to God. Despite the varied suggestions, it seems that this Lamb is a gift provided by God to deal with, take away, the world's sin (not just that of Israel – it is comprehensive in nature). It is quite likely John has in mind the lamb led to the slaughter of Isaiah 53:7, which suffered as a substitute for sin. John the Baptist could also have been thinking of the Messiah coming

---

29. By Köstenberger 2004:477, n. 67.

30. For a convenient summary see Carson 1991:149–150; Morris 1995:127–129; Ridderbos 1997:70–72.

in judgment to deal with sin, as Matthew 3:7–12 indicates. So there is judgment as well as sacrifice in this phrase. But the verb 'take away' has the notion of 'bearing off', which indicates sin being dealt with by substitution. The form of the Lamb as God's Passover Lamb is supported by the context of the Fourth Gospel's passion narrative, where in John 19:31–37 Jesus is shown to be the complete fulfilment of the Passover lamb whose bones are not to be broken. John emphasizes the truth of what happened (v. 35) and says how this fulfilled Exodus 12:46, Numbers 9:12 and Psalm 34:20. It is no coincidence that Jesus was condemned and crucified at the same time as the killing of the Passover lambs, and John would probably have seen Jesus being preserved from having his bones broken the fulfilment of the Passover.[31]

We may also note the well-known John 3:16–21 in support of this interpretation. These verses survey Jesus' complete life and indicate its purpose and meaning. The gospel message is focused on the giving of the Son for the world, so that its people may not be condemned, but by believing in him, may escape God's wrath (cf. 3:36) and have eternal life, be saved. It is possible to see the language here recalling that of Abraham *giving* his *only son*, Isaac, whom he *loved* (Gen. 22:1–14), although of course a key difference is that Abraham was spared from making this sacrifice at the last moment, but God did not spare himself (cf. Rom. 8:32). Sin was thus dealt with, but to receive forgiveness and the life of God's kingdom, belief in what Christ has done as well as in his person is required. Otherwise judgment and condemnation will follow.[32]

John 6 is also instructive on the meaning of the death of Christ. It would seem that the comment on the nearness of the Passover (v. 4) is more than a mere time reference. The Jewish Passover recalled the exodus from Egypt, and part of this celebration was

---

31. For further discussion on these and other points see Barrett 1978:175–176; Morris 1995:129–131; Carson 1991:148–151; Beasley-Murray 1991:36–39; Burge 2000:73–74; Köstenberger 2004:66–68; Keener 2003:I, 452–456.

32. See on these points the commentaries mentioned in n. 31 above and especially G. Beasley-Murray 1991:39–40.

the killing of a lamb by each household. We have seen Jesus referred to as the Lamb of God. Carson points out that the first Passover mentioned in this Gospel (2:13, 23) occurs in the context of Jesus indicating he is the temple who will be destroyed, thus pointing to his death (vv. 21–22). The third Passover (11:55–57) is at the time of his death. This one takes place close to the feeding of the five thousand, leading to the bread of life discourse, where Jesus indicates that his flesh is the true bread, which must be given for the life of the world (6:33, 51) and must be eaten for anyone to have eternal life.

> The connections become complex: the sacrifice of the lamb anticipates Jesus' death, the Old Testament manna is superseded by the real bread of life, the exodus typologically sets forth the eternal life that delivers us from sin and destruction, the Passover feast is taken over by the eucharist (both of which point to Jesus and his redemptive cross-work).[33]

As we move through this discourse, the nature of Christ's death as a sacrifice becomes even clearer. Thus John 6:40 ('For this is the will of my Father, that everyone who looks on the Son and believes in him should have eternal life, and I will raise him up on the last day') gives an analogy with John 3:16 – 'the faith in the Son that gains eternal life depends on the giving of the Son – for life and for death'.[34] Verse 51 is important: 'I am the living bread that came down from heaven. If anyone eats of this bread, he will live for ever. And the bread that I will give for the life of the world is my flesh.' It is doubtful that Jesus is making any direct reference to the Lord's Supper here.[35] But it is easy to see a connection with 1:14, the Word becoming 'flesh'. 'It is as the incarnate logos that Jesus is able to give his "flesh" for the life of the world.'[36]

But the second half of the verse must surely be interpreted as sacrificial, especially as 'if the bread of life is Jesus, what Jesus is

---

33. Carson 1991:268.
34. Beasley-Murray 1991:41.
35. This argued persuasively by Dunn 1971:328–338.
36. Moloney 1978:115, cited by Carson 1991:295.

giving is himself '.[37] The term used in *'for* the life of the world', meaning 'on behalf of' (Greek *hyper*)[38] is used elsewhere in this Gospel in a sacrificial sense. Thus 10:11, 15, 16 – Christ's death is on behalf of the sheep; in 11:50–52 – one man (Christ) dies on behalf of the people (cf. 18:14); and in 17:19 on behalf of the disciples. If it is correct to recall the Passover context through this chapter, then we are surely to see that the Bread of Life is to die as the Lamb of God for the sin of the world, for eternal life. Jesus is the one who gives his flesh voluntarily (10:17, 18). This is surely a vicarious sacrifice, recalling the Suffering Servant of Isaiah 53.

Carson sums up key points concerning the death of Christ:

> If Jesus is the Lamb of God, it is that he might take away the world's sin (1:29, 36). The slavery from which he sets men and women free is slavery to sin (8:34ff) . . . John's work is a Gospel: all the movement of the plot is towards the cross and resurrection. The cross . . . is the death of the shepherd for his sheep, the sacrifice of one man for his nation, the life that is given for the world, the victory of the Lamb of God, the triumph of the obedient Son who as a consequence of his obedience bequeaths his life, his peace, his joy, his Spirit.[39]

'Lifting up'

But as well as stressing the centrality of the death of Christ, without which people cannot receive eternal life, John also wishes to look beyond that and show how it is that the risen, ascended, exalted Christ from his throne in heaven offers the life of the age to come in the present to those who believe. A key way in which John does this is by various statements about the 'lifting up' of Jesus. We shall briefly consider their significance.[40]

---

37. Carson 1991:295. See also the valuable comments on John 6 by Dunn 1971:335–338 – 'It is the incarnate Jesus *only as given up to death* who is the bread of life' (337–338).

38. See the valuable comment on this in Morris 1995:331, n. 123.

39. Carson 1991:97.

40. In doing this, we shall make use particularly of a couple of texts:

The first reference is 3:14 ('as Moses lifted up the serpent in the wilderness, so must the Son of Man be lifted up'). Its immediate context is a reference to Christ's death, as the illustration of the lifting up of the bronze serpent indicates. It is through this action that anyone who believes in him may have eternal life (v. 15). But verse 13, in talking about the Son of Man who ascends into heaven, shows how the 'lifting up' is regarded as a decisive stage in Christ's 'journey'.[41] This lifting up on the cross is both 'the condition for and also the beginning of Jesus' ascent'.[42] John is turning the event of the cross (as 'lifting up') into a symbol indicating deeper meaning in the outward event. So this 'lifting up' of the Son of Man is the first visible part of his ascent into the heavenly realm, as well as his being established in saving power to give eternal life. This life can be accepted and experienced in union only with the living and exalted Saviour.

John 8:28 ('So Jesus said [to the Jews], "When you have lifted up the Son of Man, then you will know that I am he, and that I do nothing on my own authority, but speak just as the Father taught me') indicates that the 'lifting up' is to be the action of the Jews, presumably with the approval of the Father. God's decree is thus carried out by human means. But again one can see here more than a reference to an act of crucifixion, given the fuller context. Even though the Jews bring about Jesus' crucifixion, he cannot be destroyed, and indeed it will be a means of bringing about his glorification and enabling people to believe who he really is. Thus through this death, the Father will exalt Jesus to heaven, and those responsible for his death will afterwards come to know who he is, and what his relation to the Father is. The possibility of both judgment and salvation are indicated.

Later the Jews in wanting to crucify their king (19:15) are effectively giving him his throne. For John, the cross is the place where the kingship of Jesus is proclaimed and realized (19:19–20).

Schnackenburg 1980:II, 398–410; and Beasley-Murray 1991, ch. 3, 'The Lifting Up of the Son of Man', 34–58.

41. Schnackenburg 1980:II, 399.
42. Schnackenburg 1980:II, 399.

'It is a divine irony and paradox, hidden from unbelief, that the "king of the Jews" who has been judged and despised by men and is apparently powerless, is the true saving king (cf. 18:37; 19:5–6, 13–14).'[43]

What is taking place beyond the immediately visible is drawn out even more specifically in John 12:32. God's action is clearly seen in the 'divine passive' – he will take the Son of Man to his side, to his throne. God is also the subject of the action that will drive out the 'ruler of this world' (v. 31). 'It was through the death and exaltation of Christ that the devil was overthrown.'[44] Through Christ's exaltation on the cross and to heaven, Satan is dethroned and Jesus is enthroned.[45] But the further result of Jesus being 'lifted up' is people's salvation – that is the purpose of this action and verse 32 indicates that the one who is raised up 'from the earth' will draw people up to his exalted position, to himself as the crucified and glorified Redeemer, the one who gives them eternal life. 'Through his lifting up the saving sovereignty of God comes to the world, and the exalted Lord exercises his sovereignty as he draws all to him.'[46] Nothing can prevent this happening, and Jesus urges those who are sceptical nevertheless to believe (vv. 35–36).

The 'hour' of Jesus

Closely related to these themes is the 'hour of Jesus'. On a number of occasions, Jesus says that his hour has not yet come (2:4; 7:30; 8:20), indicating that the time of his death had not yet arrived although it was anticipated (as well as, in 2:4, indicating that he was not then ready to reveal his true identity). Other references portray his hour as 'coming' (4:21, 23; 5:25, 28; 12:27; 16:32 – in 4:23; 5:25; 12:27 and 16:32 indicating that hour is 'now here') and that it has come (12:23; 17:1), with Jesus realizing in 13:1 it had come in terms of going back to the Father.

---

43. Schnackenburg 1980:II, 400.

44. Beasley-Murray 1991:52.

45. Beasley-Murray 1991:52.

46. See Beasley-Murray 1991:52.

This 'hour' predominantly refers to Jesus' 'lifting up' on the cross, to which 12:32 gives the link. This commences in 12:23 – the hour has come 'for the Son of Man to be glorified' – and continues in verse 27, both 'hours' referring to the same matter, and indicating a theological hour rather than a temporal one.[47] So Jesus' 'hour' is both that of his death as well as of his glorification. This will take place as God wills it – the Jews cannot seize Jesus until his hour has come (cf. 7:30 and 8:20). But this hour is also one of glory, as it will lead to his glorification.

Jesus has already glorified God, as 11:4 indicates, as well as the voice in 12:28, which says that the Father has glorified his name through Jesus' ministry, and he is about to bring to a climax this glorification through Christ's submission to death and subsequent exaltation by the Father. Thus 'the glorification applies to the death-and-exaltation of Jesus – one indissoluble event'.[48] The signs have revealed his glory (2:11); Jesus' activity and ministry have revealed his Father's glory (11:40). Jesus has revealed the glory of God by obeying his will (17:4). But the 'full' glorification happens in Jesus' 'hour' (12:23), when both Father and Son are glorified (13:31).

That this hour is one of suffering and death may be seen from 12:24, where we read that just as a grain of wheat has to die in order for it to bear fruit, so also the Son of Man has to die in order for there to be many who gain eternal life. This prayer for Jesus to be glorified in his death comes through also in John 17 where Jesus asks that the giving of his life may be an acceptable sacrifice and he may then be exalted into his Father's presence in heaven (v. 5), and thus people may be given eternal life through his death and exaltation (v. 2). 'It is the Father's role to install him (Christ) in his position of heavenly power and to enable him to make his saving work bear fruit for mankind.'[49]

There is also a future glorification if Jesus' disciples bear fruit (15:8), and also when the 'Spirit of truth' glorifies Jesus (16:14). So

---

47. Schnackenburg 1980:II, 401.
48. Beasley-Murray 1991:53.
49. Schnackenburg 1980:II, 403.

these terms 'glory', 'glorify' and 'glorification' help us to appreciate not only Christ's ministry and his saving work on the cross, but also its continuation as Christ acts with God through his Spirit and in the disciples (cf. also 7:39 and 12:16).

In all this, we do of course see the Father and Son working together in the closest possible relationship. One glorifies the other, and vice versa, and this goes on through all Jesus' mission (cf. 8:54; 12:28; 17:1, 4 etc.). John 13:31–32 particularly brings this out: 'When he [Judas] had gone out, Jesus said, "Now is the Son of Man glorified, and God is glorified in him. If God is glorified in him, God will also glorify him in himself, and glorify him at once."[50] Similarly, what happens at Christ's crucifixion (the climax of what Jesus came to do: 13:1; 17:4) is also a mutual glorification, since what takes place then is, for John, both Jesus' return to the Father as well as the ascension of the Son of Man (3:13; 6:62; 13:1, 3; 16:28[51]).

Two-stage mission?

Some see in the Fourth Gospel two contrasting stages in Christ's mission: his work while he is on earth, and then his ongoing work as one who has been lifted up and glorified. John seems to acknowledge certain limits on what Jesus can do while in the flesh at that stage in

---

50. See also the perceptive comments on these two verses by Beasley-Murray 1991:53.

51. We should note the importance of the ascension here – seen also in Jesus' comment to Mary that she should not touch him, as he had not yet ascended, John 20:17, implying the essential need to return to the Father to continue his work. Stephen Smalley comments, 'Jesus not only "descends" to earth and "ascends" to heaven; he is also represented as ascending "where he was before" (John 6:62; cf. 1:1–3, et al.). In other words, the ascension is built in to every part of John's theological line. The earthly life and life-giving ministry of Jesus presupposes, in John's view, both his divine origin (before the incarnation) and his exalted destiny (after the resurrection); and with all three – the origin, life and destiny of Christ – John is deeply concerned' (Smalley 1998:267).

salvation history (e.g. not giving the Spirit until he has been glorified, 7:39), or, as Schnackenburg puts it, 'Jesus does not acquire the power to give mankind divine life until the hour of glorification.'[52] Nevertheless, John does say, 'Whoever believes in the Son has eternal life' (3:36), which was presumably true during his earthly mission through his union with the Father. Jesus perhaps anticipates his forthcoming 'lifting up' and exaltation, and on this assumption speaks thus. But we need also to keep in mind his own authority that is given him by the Father, who has told him what to say (see e.g. 5:26, 27, 30; 10:38; 17:2 etc.). Jesus' own words are 'spirit and life' (6:63, 68) and his glory is revealed in his signs. Thus perhaps one needs to beware of overdrawing this sort of contrast.[53]

Resurrection

It should be said that resurrection is also an important part of Christ's exaltation. The veiled statements of Jesus in 2:19–20 indicate the importance of the new spiritual temple to be brought about through Christ's resurrection. Jesus will take up his life again, in order for this to be so (10:17–18). The resurrection appearances in the Fourth Gospel also demonstrate the significance of what Christ continues to do in heaven. Thus we should take resurrection and exaltation together, both key parts of Christ's glorification. We should also note how the disciples understood the meaning of Jesus' puzzling, riddle-like words in 2:19 only after he was raised from the dead (2:22). Similarly, it was after describing the triumphal entry in John 12 that we read, 'when Jesus was glorified, then they remembered that these things had been written about him' (v. 16). Thus resurrection makes up part of Jesus' glorification.[54]

Conclusions

We have seen how John uses the multilayered term 'lifting up' to underline the vital significance not only of the death of Christ, but the importance of his resurrection, ascension, departure to the

---

52. Schnackenburg 1980:II, 403.

53. Schnackenburg 1980:II, 403–404.

54. These points are developed by Beasley-Murray 1991:53–56.

Father, and thus his exaltation and glorification.[55] 'Jesus is the Son of Man who has already come down from heaven, who now in the hour of his glorification, is "ascending" (3:13; 6:62), and another way of putting this is to say that he is being "lifted up" (3:14; 8:28; 12:34).'[56] Jesus has ascended into heaven and begun his saving rule. He has departed to the 'throne of God, which accomplishes the climax of the coming of God's saving sovereignty for the world'.[57] From there, the benefits of eternal life are now available to anyone who believes 'through the Spirit of the kingdom of God';[58] the benefits of the life of the age to come may be tasted in the present through this victorious ascended Christ.

Concluding summary

For John, it is essential to underline the present character of eternal life, which is due to the ministry of Christ in the world. Its future orientation is clearly seen (in verses like 4:14, 36; 6:27; 12:25; among others). But essentially, to enter life is to enter the kingdom of God (John 3:5). Enjoyment of this life in the present through belief in Christ also goes on into the future – those who receive it will live forever (6:51, 58; 8:51; 11:26). It is fair to say that John's use of 'eternal life' enables him to give greater emphasis to a present experience of salvation, maybe even at a more individual, personal level, while at the same time the essential future hope and consummation are not lost.

John 17:3 gives a succinct summary description of eternal life: it is to know God, a knowledge that goes beyond the merely theoret-

---

55. We may note also the comments of R. Bauckham on how John uses 'riddles as part of a larger literary strategy that drives readers both to think about their meaning and to read on in hope of learning their answers'. He refers to the 'lifting up' sayings as a good example of 'Johannine double-entendre' (Bauckham 2001:109).

56. Schnackenburg 1980:II, 406.

57. Beasley-Murray 1991:10.

58. Beasley-Murray 1991:10.

ical and refers to an intimate, inner communion and sharing in the life of Christ. It is he who imparts this life. Humanity left to its earthly existence (cf. 3:31b), blindness (cf. 9:39–41), captivity to sin (cf. 8:34) and the inclination to focus on what is merely transitory (cf. 6:26) is lost. Indeed, the key sin is not to believe in Jesus (16:9). It is faith in the only one who can give life (cf. 3:16) and quench deep thirst (cf. 7:37–39) that leads to this new existence that is not only for a distant future, beyond death, but for this earthly life here and now.

> Eternal life is not a static condition, but a dynamic process which includes the life of the believers in communion with Father and Son through the Spirit (14:18–21, 22–24; 15:1–17; 17:20–23) and leads to the events depicted in 5:28–29 . . . in the hour that is coming, the full impact of the decision taken now will become evident. At the resurrection of those in the tombs life and death will be revealed in all their might.[59]

While an individual aspect of receiving eternal life may be more apparent in the Fourth Gospel, there is also a focus on the community of believers who are expected to keep God's commandments as they love one another (13:12–17, 34–35: 'By this all people will know that you are my disciples, if you have love for one another'; 15:10: 'If you keep my commandments, you will abide in my love'). On this basis the world is to judge the reality and truth of their discipleship. Christ has made this love possible, but it remains a commandment. Believers will experience the hatred of the world, and must be true to Jesus in their ongoing witness (15:18–25; 16:1–4; 17:14). There is a cost to discipleship in this Gospel. But there will come a time when these things will end, as 14:1–3 (v. 3: 'And if I go and prepare a place for you, I will come again and will take you to myself, that where I am you may be also') and 17:24 ('Father, I desire that they also, whom you have given me, may be with me where I am, to see my glory') indicate. These verses may be linked with 5:28–29, 6:39, 40, 44, 54 and

---

59. De Jonge 1992:483. See also on these points Schnackenburg 1980:II, 352–354, 560–561.

12:48. Here, especially in 14:3, we have the Synoptic equivalent of the parousia, when Christ will return for his own.[60] Believers have 'a *foretaste* of the consummate reality of which 14:3 speaks . . . this is a simple, unapocalyptic representation of the coming of the Lord for the perfection of life in the kingdom of God'.[61]

This is wonderful good news, which we need to proclaim clearly. The love of God in Christ has been revealed in the whole sequence of cross–resurrection–ascension ('lifting up'). Christ is now reigning in heaven and works in the world by his Spirit and gives eternal life to all who will believe as the message is proclaimed.

When Jesus' side is pierced, leading to the effusion of blood and water (19:34), John is telling us that new life will come from this destroyed temple of his body, and we are reminded of 7:37–39, where Jesus promises that all who receive the water he offers will have streams of living water flowing from them. He was, says John, referring to the Holy Spirit, to be given after Jesus was glorified to those who believe. Water flows from Jesus' side, leading to new life. We might note the connection with Ezekiel 47, where the prophet sees water flowing from the temple, which in due course transforms the land. This is the effect Jesus' death and resurrection will have, despite the Jews' rejection of their king and destruction of their temple. The Spirit brings life, as Jesus is glorified, the life of the kingdom.[62]

It is interesting to note the other times when there is the close connection in the Fourth Gospel between water, the Spirit, life, glory and the kingdom. We see in John 3:5 how water and the Spirit together give life and entry to the kingdom of God (with a probable background of Ezekiel 36 – 37). Then in John 4, we see Jesus referring to the living water that would lead to life (4:10, 14), presumably a reference to the Spirit (cf. 4:23, 24). It is the Spirit who gives life (6:63, 68). Then, in chapter 20:22, Jesus breathes the life-giving Spirit on his disciples (cf. Gen. 2:7 and Ezek. 37),

---

60. See on these issues de Jonge 1992:484–486.
61. Beasley-Murray 1991:11.
62. Leithart 2000:261–262, where some of these points are elaborated.

imparting to them his resurrection life, connected with his glorification through the cross and resurrection. Thus again we see the intimate connection between life and the kingdom of God, as well as a 'present' or 'inaugurated' aspect to this life.

So we conclude that to have eternal life is to have life in the kingdom of God. You cannot have this life without being in the kingdom. To have this life is to acknowledge that Christ is king, that he rules over his kingdom. Despite the actions of the Jews, Jesus is in control. God gives life through the glorified Christ. The events of this Gospel have inexorably been leading up to Christ's 'lifting up', resurrection, ascension and exaltation. His hour has been coming and now is. To acknowledge God's sovereignty is to be part of his kingdom. There can be no gospel for John without presenting Christ as Lord, as King, the one who gives life, and who admits people to his kingdom, this kingdom from above, *on his terms*, that of being born from above by his Spirit. Any other way leads to death, as the forces that oppose Jesus remind us (e.g. John 8:23, 24, 44; 10:5, 8, 10, 12, 13 – the false shepherds; Pilate and the Jewish authorities of John 18 and 19).

When preaching eternal life, it is important to set it in this kingdom framework of Christ as King and Lord. Eternal life is not merely a free gift that people should be urged to accept, but it needs to be presented with the various demands of discipleship. There is no eternal life without understanding Christ as the one who has full authority, for he is Lord and King.

4. THE KING, HIS KINGDOM AND THE GOSPEL: MATTHEW, MARK AND LUKE-ACTS

Chris Green

Introduction

The task in this chapter is to look at the kingdom of God in the writings of Matthew, Mark and Luke, and to explore how the kingdom relates to the gospel, and whether preaching the kingdom is to engage in a different activity from preaching the cross. If the answer is 'yes', we might then fruitfully ask whether one or another way might be more suitable in a given context and given the profile of a particular audience. If the answer is 'no', then we shall need to engage in some re-evaluation of contemporary practice, not only among those who do see it as a viable alternative, but also among those who do not and who therefore shy away from any kind of reference to the kingdom as if it were inherently flawed.

I want to begin in an unusual place, by looking at the second volume of Luke's theology of the kingdom, the book of Acts.[1] I highlight it particularly because since it is neither a Synoptic nor a

---

1. For a more developed account of my view of Acts see Green 2005.

Johannine Gospel, nor a Pauline epistle, it is frequently thrust
into the shadows on this subject, and therefore its distinctive contribution is, at best, marginalized and, at worst, assumed to be
non-existent.[2] It was the early observation of James D. G. Dunn,
for instance, in contrasting Luke's Gospel with Acts, that

> Where the Spirit had been so little bestowed (before Pentecost) the
> message of the Kingdom was more appropriate. Where the Spirit had
> been bestowed in greater measure (after Pentecost) there was no need to
> speak in such veiled terms . . . [A]ccording to Luke the early church was
> so full of the Spirit that talk both of the Kingdom and of its still future
> aspect for the most part faded into the background, and the direct,
> immediate experience of the Spirit took central place.[3]

But the evidence points in the opposite direction to Dunn's view.
Without minimizing the central role of the Spirit, it becomes clear
that Acts has a sharp and unique contribution to make on the
kingdom. Rather than having 'faded into the background' under the
pressure of a diminished eschatological expectation, the kingdom
turns out to be a major concern of Luke's work.

---

2. I have not attempted the complex task of showing the interrelationship
   between the theology of Acts and the theology of Luke's Gospel. Much
   work remains to be done here, especially as they are simultaneously
   discrete, sequential, overlapping and superimposed. There are elements of
   continuity, discontinuity and fulfilment that commentaries on one or
   other cannot have as major concerns. Tannehill 1990 has served us well
   here, but I suspect his impact has been more felt in the field of Acts or
   Luke than that of Luke-Acts, a rarer specialism.
3. Dunn 1970a:39f. This early observation is illuminating for the
   consequences in Dunn's own thinking, for which see the critique in
   David Peterson's chapter in this volume.

Acts and the kingdom of God

The kingdom of God

Although the phrase 'the kingdom of God' occurs infrequently in Acts, it occurs at critically important points. Since the ground-breaking work of Richard Tannehill, *The Narrative Unity of Luke-Acts*,[4] Acts studies are becoming increasingly sensitive to Luke's literary strategies, one of which is the careful placing of significant motifs.[5] For our purposes, the opening and closing of Acts are important.

The opening scene, Acts 1:3–11

The opening section of Acts shows the risen Jesus in intense debate with his disciples, as he instructs them further about his and their future ministries as a consequence of his death and resurrection. He set the discussion running by appearing to his disciples over forty days *and speaking about the kingdom of God* (1:3). It appears that *the kingdom* can function as a headline over his teaching. Because of the necessary implication of his being the prophesied Davidic Messiah, which Luke will spell out throughout Acts, their question is entirely natural: 'Lord, will you at this time restore the kingdom to Israel?' (1:6). That is, will you now reunite the two halves of the divided and exiled Davidic monarchy in a new and explicit expression of God's rule in this land? The double question of timing ('at this time') and place ('to Israel') obviously show their excitement and enthusiasm, even though a correction of the understanding is called for.

Jesus replies to both questions, 'It is not for you to know times or seasons that the Father has fixed by his own authority. But you will receive power when the Holy Spirit has come upon you' (vv. 7, 8). The timing of God's plans is for him alone to know, but there has been a clear step forward in what has just happened, and another is about to come in the giving of the Spirit. If the disciples were thinking of the next stage of God's plan as the final events in the history of the world, they have to learn that it is merely the beginning of a

---

4. Tannehill 1990.

5. Insights which show how seminal Tannehill's work has been have informed a number of the essays in Marshall and Peterson 1998.

grand new era. Similarly, the scope of the *kingdom* is larger than they can imagine. Jerusalem was the centre of rule for the Davidic king, but that will no longer be true. Jesus is that king, but he will rule from a heavenly throne, over the whole earth. And so the witnesses to his resurrection majesty will not merely stay in the erstwhile royal capital, but go to 'all Judea and Samaria', the two halves of the divided monarchy. The first act of the new king is to reunite his kingdom. Judea and Samaria are not two separate countries, but a broken whole, like the old divided West and East Germany. We could almost put hyphens in Jesus' speech: 'First go to my kingdom of Judea-and-Samaria, and then go to my new kingdom, which extends to *the end of the earth*.' This global reign will continue until, to quote the angel, 'Jesus, who was taken up from you into heaven, will come in the same way as you saw him go into heaven' (v. 11).

So the centre of the kingdom, in the sense of the place from which the king rules, is relocated to heaven, and this rule both fulfils and replaces the political or revolutionary hopes for the overthrow of Roman government. The disciples may have hoped that the reign of Jesus would mean that Caesar would no longer rule over Jerusalem or Palestine; it actually means Caesar no longer rules anywhere.

The closing scene: Acts 28:17–31

The initial double mention of the kingdom (1:3, 6) is echoed at the end of Acts. Paul, under house arrest in Rome, continued his preaching and teaching to any crowd he could gather. Twice in the closing verses, Luke summarizes the message Paul taught. Speaking to the Jews in Rome, Paul 'expounded to them, testifying to the kingdom of God and trying to convince them about Jesus both from the Law of Moses and from the Prophets' (Acts 28:23). And more generally, in the conclusion to the entire book, Luke reports that Paul spent his time 'proclaiming the kingdom of God and teaching about the Lord Jesus Christ with all boldness and without hindrance' (v. 31).

Luke's careful placement of a double mention of the kingdom at both ends of the book must surely mean that, in his understanding, everything that happens in between functions as an explanation and exposition of that theme, and that the message of the kingdom is one valid summary of the content of the book. So we need to follow the theme through and see how it develops.

Philip: Acts 8:4–40

Philip's ministry encompasses the gospel travelling outside the strict racial enclaves that until then had kept the gospel among Jews, opening the second phase described in Acts 1:8. The Samaritans were the disobedient, rebellious half of the divided monarchy who had built their own alternative temple (1 Kgs 12), and the Ethiopian would have been excluded from the authentic temple by his physical impairment and possibly by his race, too (Deut. 23:1–8).[6] The inclusion of both Samaritans and a eunuch as the motif of Philip's ministry shows Luke's exposition of the widening embrace of the gospel. We need to note that at this important moment, the phrase used to summarize the Samaritans' response to Philip's preaching was that 'when they believed Philip as he preached good news about the kingdom of God and the name of Jesus Christ, they were baptized, both men and women' (8:12). 'Jesus Christ' is used here, as throughout Acts, in its full biblical–theological sense of Jesus-the-Davidic-Messiah.[7] So, Luke's emphasis, in this stage of the fulfilment of Acts 1:8, is that news of the kingly rule of Jesus was taken to Samaria and beyond.

Paul and Barnabas: Acts 14:19–23

Paul and Barnabas' first missionary journey had taken them from Antioch, via Cyprus, to Perga, Pisidian Antioch and continued to Derbe. With the possible exception of Perga, every stop involved pioneer evangelism.[8] The return journey involved revisiting those new churches and encouraging them, or as Luke reports it,

> they returned to Lystra and to Iconium and to Antioch, strengthening
> the souls of the disciples, encouraging them to continue in the faith, and
> saying that through many tribulations we must enter the kingdom of
> God. And when they had appointed elders for them in every church,

---

6. For the place of Gentiles in Israel see the thoughtful and provocative
   study of Hays 2003.

7. Acts 2:38; 3:6; 4:10; 8:12; 9:34; 10:36, 48; 11:17; 15:26; 16:18; 20:21; 28:31.

8. Perga is particularly mentioned in 14:25 on the return trip. Had the dispute
   with John Mark (13:13) deflected them from evangelism on the outward leg?

with prayer and fasting they committed them to the Lord in whom they had believed (21b–23).

In other words, although 'the kingdom of God' is useful short-hand for the evangelistic message, as in Philip's ministry, it is not exhausted by that, and is here a future hope for (Gentile) Christians – and especially Christian leaders – which is supposed to encourage us as we face persecution. Jesus' kingdom is now fully racially inclusive but still future oriented (1:11). In Luke's literary strategy, it is evident that this second message for new Christians is as normative as the first.

Jews and Gentiles: Acts 19:8–10

A further important summary sequence of Paul's ministry occurs in the Ephesian phase, where Paul spent a more extended period of time, perhaps because of the significance of the place, or at least the fast turnover of his audience. Paul

> entered the synagogue and for three months spoke boldly, reasoning and persuading them about the kingdom of God. But when some became stubborn and continued in unbelief, speaking evil of the Way before the congregation, he withdrew from them and took the disciples with him, reasoning daily in the hall of Tyrannus. This continued for two years, so that all the residents of Asia heard the word of the Lord, both Jews and Greeks (vv. 8–10).

Unless we assume Luke means that Paul changed his message as he moved from synagogue to debating hall, this whole period of time, engaging with both Jews and Gentiles, is covered by the one rubric. So extended speaking, reasoning and persuading, over a two-year period – the area we might consider to be more apologetics than evangelism – is also part of Luke's theology of the *kingdom*.

Christians and their leaders: Acts 20:18–35

Although Luke frequently shows Paul caring for the churches he has planted and the leaders he has placed, there is only one occasion where he tells us exactly what Paul did and said, and that is in the speech to the Ephesian elders in Miletus (20:18–35). Luke's pattern of writing must mean that this is intended to be a typical, not eccentric, pattern.

Once again we are presented with a summary, and within the entire speech a one-sentence distillation of three years' work: 'I know that none of you among whom I have gone about proclaiming the kingdom will see my face again' (20:25). Paul's entire and extended ministry to Christians, and to Christian leaders in particular, is summarized in terms of the *kingdom*. That this is not a narrow concept is shown by the occurrence of a near synonym a few words later: 'I did not shrink from declaring to you the whole counsel of God' (20:27).

So here the *kingdom of God* is a term that encompasses every aspect of Christian doctrine and discipleship, and the necessary qualifications for and activities of Christian leadership, both positively, in proclaiming the gospel, and negatively, in the battle with false teaching.

In Luke's strategy, then, Acts 19:8–10 describes the summary of Paul's uninterrupted ministry to non-Christians, and 20:18–35, his uninterrupted ministry to Christian leaders. Both should be seen as Paul's normal, or at least intended, pattern. That both can be explained under the heading of *the kingdom* shows how important, and conceptually rich, this term is.

Preaching the kingdom: Acts 28:23–31

It should not surprise us, then, that Luke uses the terms 'testifying' to the kingdom of God' (28:23) and 'proclaiming the kingdom' (28:31) as adequate summaries of Paul's ministry in Rome. The phrase includes evangelism and apologetics, church planting and strengthening, leadership development and modelling. It is a valid summary of Luke's message: this is how the kingly rule of Jesus is played out.

That 'kingly rule' is the most critical and easily missed part of the concept, because, as the spotlight shifts from the visible ministry of Jesus before his ascension to the visible obedience of the church after it, there is a danger that the 'kingdom' is understood in a way detached from the 'king', which would be disastrous. There is no sense in which Jesus, by being in heaven, is absent from earth, or that the church in some of its activities replaces him. Jesus is the active ruler over his kingdom, and the building and equipping of his church is exactly what his kingly rule is designed to produce until his return in glory.

In fact, we can go further. Of the eight references to the kingdom in Acts, five come in the context of 'preaching the kingdom of God', or some such phrase.[9] Given the significance of the placing of those terms, that means that an extraordinary weight of emphasis is being placed on the verbal communication of the 'good news (*euangelion*) about the kingdom of God' (8:12). Luke's emphasis is so often understood to be on the action in Acts that insufficient weight is placed on speaking, yet on numerous occasions it is speaking which is the distinctive outward-facing activity of the church.[10] Something like 20% of the book is reported speech, in nineteen sermons, addresses and defences. That the emphasis in the kingdom references falls on *preaching* the kingdom should not surprise us. Furthermore, that is entirely of a piece with the material in Luke, where he uses the same distinctive phrase.[11] Kevin Giles rightly observes that 'In both the third Gospel and in Acts the preaching of the Kingdom is the proclamation of the future advent of God's reign which can be experiencially [sic] and personally known now through repentance and faith.'[12] That observation moves us on.

The kingdom and the king

It is being increasingly demonstrated that the theology of Acts is often worked out not only in its narrative, but also in its Christology,[13] and that is obviously true with regard to a major

---

9. 8:12; 19:8; 20:25; 28:23, 31.

10. 4:29, 31; 6:2, 4; 8:4, 14, 25; 11:1; 13:5, 7, 44, 46, 48; 14:25; 15:35, 36; 16:6, 32; 17:13; 18:11; 19:10; 20:32.

11. Luke 4:43; 8:1; 9:2, 60; 16:16.

12. Giles 1981:67. The structural emphasis we have observed must qualify Giles's frequency-based observation that 'The infrequent appearance in Acts of the terms (sic) the Kingdom of God immediately shows it is less important here than in the gospel' (Giles 1981:66). In fact, I think Giles's own article undermines his observation, showing how central the concept is, linked as it is with the kingly reign of the risen Jesus.

13. See, for instance, Hans F. Bayer, 'The Preaching of Peter in Acts', in Marshall

theme like the *kingdom*. Luke deploys a range of titles to describe Jesus' current reign, and although they do not use the words 'king' or 'kingdom', they provide necessary content.

Leader

Acts describes Jesus as *archēgos*, the leader or pre-eminent one, on two occasions in Peter's speeches. In chapter 3, after a beggar has been healed, Peter explained to the crowd that he is not the source of the man's new health, but rather it is the risen Jesus who has acted. He attributes to Jesus a range of titles:

> The God of Abraham, the God of Isaac, and the God of Jacob, the God of our fathers, glorified his *servant* Jesus, whom you delivered over and denied in the presence of Pilate, when he had decided to release him. But you denied the *Holy and Righteous One,* and asked for a murderer to be granted to you, and you killed the *Author of life,* whom God raised from the dead. To this we are witnesses. And his *name* – by faith in his *name* – has made this man strong whom you see and know, and the faith that is through Jesus has given the man this perfect health in the presence of you all.
>
> And now, brothers, I know that you acted in ignorance, as did also your rulers. But what God foretold by the mouth of all the prophets, that his *Christ* would suffer, he thus fulfilled. Repent therefore, and turn again, that your sins may be blotted out, that times of refreshing may come from the presence of the Lord, and that he may send the *Christ* appointed for you, Jesus, whom heaven must receive until the time for restoring all the things about which God spoke by the mouth of his holy prophets long ago. Moses said, 'The Lord God will raise up for you *a prophet* like me from your brothers. You shall listen to him in whatever he tells you. And it shall be that every soul who does not listen to that prophet shall be destroyed from the people.' And all the prophets who have spoken, from Samuel and those who came after him, also proclaimed these days. You are the sons of the prophets and of the covenant that God made with your fathers, saying to Abraham,

---

and Peterson (1998: 257–274) and, with particular reference to soteriology, David Peterson, 'Atonement Theology in Luke-Acts: Some Methodological Reflections', in Williams, Clarke, Head and Instone-Brewer 2004: 56–71.

'And in your offspring shall all the families of the earth be blessed.'
God, having raised up *his servant,* sent him to you first, to bless you by
turning every one of you from your wickedness (3:13–26; my italics).

Each of those titles is worth exploring in relation to our theme,
but in the context of Peter's message the title that is particularly
prominent, because of its irony, is the *Author (archēgos) of life* who
was *killed* in exchange for a *murderer,* but whom *God raised from the
dead.* Jesus' pre-eminence, therefore, is over everything living,
because he is placed in a position of creative authority over everything else: he has an inherent right to rule everything living
because he created life itself.

Peter's second use of the *archēgos* title gives a rather different
flavour:

> The God of our fathers raised Jesus, whom you killed by hanging him
> on a tree. God exalted him at his right hand as *Leader* [there's the word]
> and Saviour, to give repentance to Israel and forgiveness of sins. And we
> are witnesses to these things, and so is the Holy Spirit, whom God has
> given to those who obey him (5:30–32).

In this passage the title is not an inherent one that is proper to
Jesus from all eternity as Creator, but one that was given to him
after his resurrection, and which is proper to him as Saviour,
which means the one who gives 'repentance . . . and forgiveness of
sins'.[14] In both understandings he is the rightful ruler, but the
importance of the first is that Jesus is the ruler over all people,
irrespective of whether they have come to him as Saviour.

At God's right hand

The title *leader* was given to Jesus when God exalted him *at his right
hand,* and that spatial language also underscores Jesus' right to reign.
Repeatedly in Acts *God's right hand* is given as the place to which

---

14. The phrase *to Israel* must be understood as a reference to Peter's
   contemporary audience; any interpretation that limited salvation to Israel
   would fail to convince in the wider context of Acts.

Jesus ascended, from where he rules, and from whence he will return.[15] It is a position of absolute and unassailable authority, over everything and everyone whom his messengers will encounter. It is the place of enthronement, and of personally inhabited kingship. As with the related term *heaven*, there is no idea of distance or remoteness in the language, as if Jesus were in some sense absent because he is at God's right hand. Rather, precisely because he is there he has the right to be present everywhere, intimately, and to supervise the spreading of the gospel. 'This Jesus God raised up, and of that we all are witnesses. Being therefore exalted at the right hand of God, and having received from the Father the promise of the Holy Spirit, he has poured out this that you yourselves are seeing and hearing' (2:32–34).

David

The greatest exemplar of the Old Testament monarchy, and the pattern for the ideal successor, was King David. The understanding that Jesus was this successor, who was greater even than David himself, is a key part of the unfolding Christology of Acts, and is referred to explicitly on nine occasions.[16] The picture emerges of a superior successor, who although he was David's Son was also God's Son, and therefore although he was David's descendant was also his Lord. This is, of course, deeply dependent on a Christological reading of the Psalms that is widespread in the New Testament and which Luke himself traces back to Jesus (Luke 24:44–49).

Lord

The most frequent title given to Jesus in Acts is *Lord*, whether in the simple title *the Lord*, the fuller *the Lord Jesus* or the complete *The Lord Jesus Christ*.[17] *Lord* is a title which Luke also gives clearly to

---

15. Acts 2:25, 33; 2:34; 3:7; 5:31; 7:55, 56.

16. Acts 2:25, 29, 34; 4:25; 13:22 (*2), 34, 36; 15:16). There are other references to David in Acts that are not explicitly linked to Luke's Christology.

17. Acts 1:6, 21, 24; 2:25, 34, 36, 47; 4:33; 5:9, 14, 19; 7:59f; 8:16, 22, 24ff, 39; 9:1, 5, 10f, 13, 15, 17, 27f, 31, 35, 42; 10:4, 14, 33, 36; 11:8, 16f, 20f, 23f; 12:7, 11, 17, 23; 13:2, 10ff, 44, 47ff; 14:3, 23; 15:11, 17(?), 26, 35f, 40; 16:14f,

God the Father, and which the Father shares with and bestows on the Son. Luke makes this clear in Peter's Pentecost sermon, as he quotes from Psalm 110:

> The Lord said to my Lord,
> Sit at my right hand,
>> until I make your enemies your footstool (Acts 2:34–5).

Again, a high Christology is imported from the Psalms, and the title is unambiguous. Jesus is not God the Father, but shares everything with the Father other than that. 'God has made him both Lord and Christ, this Jesus whom you crucified' (Acts 2:36). This transference of authority is developed in the structure of the sermon, which begins with an offer from Joel, that 'everyone who calls upon the name of the Lord shall be saved' (Acts 2:21) and ends by explaining that the *name* of the Lord they are to call on for salvation is Jesus (2:38). *Name* is quite clearly a synonym for divine title,[18] and there is again the transference of royal privilege as Jesus takes on the right to call a people his own people, called by his *name*.[19]

The Lord Jesus Christ

The climactic summary of Acts 28:31 should therefore strike us the harder in the light of this evidence. It is not just that Paul preaches the *kingdom*, but that he was *proclaiming the kingdom of God and teaching about the Lord Jesus Christ* – and the full weight of those titles should be noted. Jesus is a monarch, and with a realm of his own. That realm is the whole of creation, and all things living are subject to him and accountable before him.

31f; 18:8f, 25; 19:5, 10, 13, 17, 20; 20:19, 21, 24, 35; 21:13f; 22:8, 10, 19; 23:11; 26:15; 28:31. It is increasingly difficult as Acts progresses to discern where Luke is making a distinction between Jesus and God the Father, as the former takes over the biblical roles of the latter.

18. Acts 2:21, 38; 3:6, 16; 4:7, 10, 12, 17f, 30; 5:28, 40f; 8:12, 16; 9:14ff, 21, 27f; 10:43, 48; 16:18; 19:5, 13, 17; 21:13; 22:16; 26:9.

19. Acts 15:14, 17.

The kingdom and the gospel

How, then, are the gospel and the kingdom related? That they are related is quite clear, for Philip 'preached good news [i.e. he gospelled] about the kingdom of God and the name of Jesus Christ' (8:12).[20] We have seen how a concept like *name* is linked to forgiveness of sins and the gift of the Spirit (2:38), remembering how in Acts the titles of Jesus often explain the unstated theology.[21] We have also seen how *kingdom* in Acts is a rich field of meaning that, at its maximum, can be coterminous with 'the whole counsel of God' (20:25–27), and *the gospel* is a standard Lukan phrase for the Christian message.[22]

In view of the flexibility of the terms, perhaps it is best to see the distinctive contribution of Acts' way of talking about the *kingdom* in this way. It is not a separate message from the gospel, because whether the early church proclaimed the finished work, royal titles, kingly rule or universal judgment of the Lord Jesus, they are all organically related, and merely perspectives from which to view the whole. *Kingdom's* contribution, in Acts, is twofold. It stresses first the present and future lordship of God,[23] with the necessary focus on the present reign of the Lord-King Jesus, of his right to rule, of his coming Father-endorsed judgment based on his cross and resurrection, and of the glorious delight that he calls men and women to repent and believe in him, and to receive forgiveness and the gift of the Spirit. That is, to live rightly under his rule. As Kevin Giles has noted, 'the Word proclaimed is well nigh equated with the risen Jesus'.[24] Second, *Kingdom* stresses the present and future realms of his lordship, with growing numbers of men and women from all nations coming under his loving reign, with a right to claim lordship over everyone living and dead being now announced but in the future validated, and with (ulti-

---

20. Luke 4:43; 8:1; 16:16.
21. So *Servant* (Acts 3:13, 26; 4:25, 27, 30) clearly has a substitutionary, and I would argue a *penal* substitutionary, meaning inherited from the Servant Songs of Isaiah.
22. Acts 8:25, 40; 14:7, 21; 15:7; 16:10; 20:24.
23. By 'God' here I mean the Trinity, not the Father alone.
24. Giles 1982:17.

mately) the whole of creation being remade under his throne. *Kingdom*, then, does not explain the means by which this comes to pass, for which Luke has other terms, but it explains the glorious consequences of the royal obedience of the Son of God.[25]

Mark and the kingdom of God

Moving to the Gospels themselves we do come to more natural territory for the theme of the kingdom. It is often noted as a, if not the, dominant note of Jesus' preaching, and as such a characteristic element it can be used as a criterion of authenticity. I want here to look at only one of the three Synoptic Gospels, Mark, and, rather than conduct a widespread analysis of his theology of the kingdom, to apply three of the lessons that we have learnt from studying Acts; namely (1) that the strategic placement of teaching is an indicator of its importance; (2) that the openings and closings of these books are often indicators of importance; and (3) that we need to consider not merely the word 'kingdom', but other overlapping words, the 'semantic domain'[26] or 'lexical field', such as the terms *Lord*, *Christ* and *God's right hand* we studied there.

The final mention of the kingdom in Mark

Because the concept of the kingdom is rightly so associated with Jesus' teaching, and especially his parables, it would be dangerously easy to locate it there exclusively. It is not difficult to find help in outlining Jesus' theology of the kingdom from his teaching

---

25. I think, therefore, that what R. T. France has called the 'scholarly consensus' that 'kingdom' means the act of ruling in the abstract, excluding entirely any concrete sense, or realm, needs some qualification. See France 1990:12. It is noteworthy that some scholars are beginning to say that the idea includes *both* rule *and* realm. See Ulrich Luz's comments in Balz and Schneider 1990:201, and Graeme L. Goldsworthy's in Alexander and Rosner 2000:617. I am grateful to an Oak Hill student, Chris Thomson, for this observation.

26. See Louw and Nida 1992.

and practice. It is, after all, his opening message, 'The time is fulfilled, and the kingdom of God is at hand; repent and believe in the gospel' (Mark 1:15), and we note how *kingdom* and *gospel* are connected. But Mark is not a naive writer, and he shares the literary strategy of identifying a term, and then suffusing it with his preferred meaning. This inevitably involves looking outside one moment or strand of the gospel into the work in its entirety, and I want to focus here on the final mention of the kingdom in Mark's Gospel, which occurs once Jesus has died:

> Joseph of Arimathea, a respected member of the Council, *who was also himself looking for the kingdom of God*, took courage and went to Pilate and asked for the body of Jesus. Pilate was surprised to hear that he should have already died. And summoning the centurion, he asked him whether he was already dead. And when he learned from the centurion that he was dead, he granted the corpse to Joseph. And Joseph bought a linen shroud, and taking him down, wrapped him in the linen shroud and laid him in a tomb that had been cut out of the rock. And he rolled a stone against the entrance of the tomb (Mark 15:43–46).

That note on Joseph's motivation in claiming Jesus' body is a critical piece of the jigsaw giving Mark's understanding of the kingdom. Quite clearly, the kingdom cannot be seen as something that has no further relevance once Jesus has died. It is not a failed enterprise. Nor is it something which, Jesus having died, has been introduced in its fullness. No. God's kingdom requires both the death and resurrection of Jesus to inaugurate it. In a moment we shall look briefly at some of the Old Testament roots for that belief, but for now it is enough to ponder what else Joseph could have been, as Mark puts it, *looking for* (v. 43), if not the resurrection of the King? In what other sense could the kingdom still be future for him, bearing in mind that the actual possession of a physical corpse is at stake? This certainly ties in with Mark's rich, but often unnoticed, theology of resurrection.[27]

---

27. The three famous cross predictions are also resurrection predictions
  (8:31; 9:31; 10:33, 34), but other predictions are woven into the narrative

The final mention of the king in Mark

Moving outside the word 'kingdom' brings us to its near neighbour, 'king'. Again it is a term that has occurred earlier in the
Gospel and the description of Jesus' rival monarchy to Herod's
(6:14–44 describes two royal feasts)[28] has shown itself to be a pow-
erful and charged one. Jesus has claimed similar royal titles of *Lord*
(12:36), *Son of David* and *Christ* (8:29), *Son of Man* (10:33) throughout the narrative, and even claimed to be the *Son* of Isaiah's
vineyard owner (12:1–10; cf. Isa. 5:1–7).

But *king* is a particularly debated term in Jesus' trial before Pilate
(15:2), the choice of the people (15:9, 12) and Jesus' torture (15:18).
This concentrated reminder of the title serves to highlight it before
the climax: the crucifixion, where 'the inscription of the charge
against him read, "The King of the Jews"' (15:26). Mark's irony

---

as well (9:9; 12:1–11, especially the climax, 14:25, 27–28). It should be
noted too that Jesus disputed the Sadducees' lack of theology of
resurrection (12:18–27) and seems to have presupposed it in his messianic
self-understanding (5:41–42; 12:10–11). Arguably, even the parables of
ch. 4 have a pattern of insignificance preceding glory. Mark underlines the
genuineness of Jesus' death eight times in 15:37–47, and underlines that
the same women witnessed Jesus' death (15:40), burial (15:47) and the
empty tomb (16:1). Peter Bolt has noted particularly sharply how Jesus'
enemy in the Gospels, as the power which holds men and women in its
thrall until Jesus releases them, is *death* (9:26–27), and release comes by
means of the cross and resurrection; see especially ch. 2 of Bolt 2004. It
emerges that there is a much deeper resource here than an apparent 'lack'
of an ending might suggest. For myself, *pace* a number of eminent
evangelical commentators, I find that 16:8 makes a satisfactory ending
for the Gospel, precisely because it makes the reader reread from the
beginning and re-evaluate all the resurrection material.

28. Note, too, that Herod's royal feast is the occasion for John's death,
prefiguring both Jesus' destiny and that of the Twelve, whose mission
frames this story, but also that this scene is a flashback to explain Herod's
view of Jesus, which was that some had said 'John the Baptist has been
raised from the dead' (6:14). Cross, resurrection and kingdom combine
even in this small scene.

allows as to see this inscription as both humanity's verdict (that Jesus is a pretender) and God's (that he is genuine), that what one group intends as a lie is actually the truth, that what they intend as the end is actually the beginning, and what they intend as a humiliation is actually a triumph. This is the way the king enters his kingdom. At the triumphal entry into Jerusalem the crowds had shouted, 'Hosanna! Blessed is he who comes in the name of the Lord! Blessed is the coming kingdom of our father David! Hosanna in the highest!' (11:9–10). They expected Jesus' arrival to bring in the kingdom, and they quoted Psalm 118:25, 26 in support. That is the same psalm that Jesus used as the climax to the parable of the tenants, 'The stone that the builders rejected / has become the cornerstone; / this was the Lord's doing, / and it is marvellous in our eyes' (12:10–11, quoting Ps. 118:10–11), where the motif of rejection and exaltation must apply to the murder of the son in the story and therefore to his (i.e. Jesus') subsequent vindication. It is striking that if Mark's hints are followed and Psalm 118 is referred to, we discover that the journey ends with the words:

> Bind the festal sacrifice with cords,
>   up to the horns of the altar! (Ps. 118:27).

Jesus' accusers speak more than they know, therefore, when they crucify him as *The King of the Jews*. Sacrificial crucifixion was exactly what this king expected, along with his subsequent vindication.

Hence the poignancy, so often noted, of the final reference to the king in Mark: 'the chief priests with the scribes mocked him to one another, saying, "He saved others; he cannot save himself. Let the Christ, the King of Israel, come down now from the cross that we may see and believe"' (15:31–32). The choice lies at the very point they unwittingly highlight: it is precisely because he does not save himself that he can, and does, save others, and this is the wonder of how *the Christ, the King of Israel* governs his kingdom.

For Mark, then, three elements which are usually separated need to come together: an understanding of the kingdom, which is richer than merely the teaching in the parables; an understanding of the cross as the moment of enthronement of the king; and an understanding of resurrection as the vindication of the king.

One final example should serve to show how persistently inter-locked those elements are in Mark:

> And as they were eating, (Jesus) took bread, and after blessing it broke it
> and gave it to them, and said, 'Take; this is my body.' And he took a cup,
> and when he had given thanks he gave it to them, and they all drank of it.
> And he said to them, 'This is my blood of the covenant, which is poured
> out for many. Truly, I say to you, I will not drink again of the fruit of the
> vine until that day when I drink it new in the kingdom of God' (14:22–25).

Notice how the three elements emerge: God's kingdom is to be brought about by Jesus' death, to benefit others. But Jesus' death will not be the end of him, for he will drink wine again at some celebratory point in the future. Kingdom, death and resurrection are connected concepts.

The entry of the king in Mark

We began eccentrically, at the end of Mark's Gospel precisely because the material on the kingdom from the beginning is so famil-iar.[29] In the light of the importance of the kingdom of God at the end, however, it should strike with new force that Jesus' first words are, 'The time is fulfilled, and the kingdom of God is at hand' (1:15), and he personally brings in that reign of God as God's Son (1:1).[30] The miracles are therefore an exercising of his rightful rule over all creation, and his imposing of the right order under God – which includes the way he extends mercy to ex-rebels. But beginning at the end means we can underline that the kingdom of God is not a different theological motif to the cross, the resurrection, and sin-bearing, nor is it one that can be chosen as an alternative model to develop to a less guilt-ridden culture without any messy problems

---

29. See, for instance, the relevant sections in Beasley-Murray 1986;
    Caragounis 1992b; France 1990; Ladd 1974; Marshall 1990; Willis 1987
    gives a useful and thorough survey.

30. Mark underlines that title by ensuring we hear it from the disciples (8:38),
    from Jesus (14:61–62), from his defeated demonic opponents (5:7) and
    from God himself (1:11; 9:7).

about punishment or corpses. In that sense, we must endorse an important conclusion by Professor Chrys Caragounis of the University of Lund, in Sweden. In a very stimulating article Caragounis argues that

> the concept of the kingdom of God is parallel with the Johannine concept of eternal life . . . and the Pauline concept of Salvation. Precisely as those who have put their faith in the atoning work of Christ are said to possess eternal life, to be in Christ, or to be saved, in spite of the fact that eternal life or salvation . . . are essentially eschatological concepts, so also believers may be said to have entered into the kingdom of God despite the fact that the kingdom of God, like eternal life and salvation, can be properly experienced only at the end of time.[31]

Matthew and Luke and the kingdom of God

Rather than survey all the material in the Gospel that mentions the kingdom, or engage with all the vast contemporary literature on this subject, I want at this point to do something much more modest: to visit the one passage in Matthew and Luke which could most plausibly be advanced as teaching that the kingdom is inaugurated in some other way than the cross,[32] most probably by his

---

31. Caragounis 1992b:425. We shall return to Caragounis's article below.
32. Space precludes visiting the other notorious passage, Luke 17:20. There are numerous finely balanced arguments to be weighed there over the meaning of *entos hymōn estin* (is among you), but if we were pursuing the issues pertinent to this chapter I would note that any conclusion reached there must take into account that contextually the kingdom of God is again tied to the title Son of Man (17:22), which is immediately linked with the cross (17:25). Since I support Caragounis so strongly in what follows it is only fair to note that I am less persuaded by him on this verse, and on this point follow the critique of Darrell L. Bock, 'The Kingdom of God in New Testament Theology: The Battle, The Christ, The Spirit-Bearer, and Returning Son of Man', in Baker 2001; although, since Bock writes as a 'Dispensationalist with a Small "d" ' (*JETS* 41 [1998]:383–396), and I am

presence, teaching or action, and I will discuss it in the light of Caragounis's article.[33]

Matthew 12:25–28 (Luke 11:17–20)

> Knowing their thoughts, (Jesus) said to them, 'Every kingdom divided against itself is laid waste, and no city or house divided against itself will stand. And if Satan casts out Satan, he is divided against himself. How then will his kingdom stand? And if I cast out demons by Beelzebul, by whom do your sons cast them out? Therefore they will be your judges. But if it is by the Spirit of God that I cast out demons, then the kingdom of God has come upon you.

The critical phrase here is the one translated by the last four words, 'has come upon you' (ephthasen); and it is so important because, as Caragounis says,

> it is the only kingdom saying in the synoptics that apparently describes the kingdom of God as having arrived . . . If the Kingdom of God has come already, say, by the time Jesus uttered the saying . . ., how is the remainder of Jesus' earthly existence to be understood? And what about the Son of man's duty to 'give his life as a ransom for many'? What is the significance of his death? And how did Jesus relate his death to the kingdom of God?[34]

Those are excellent questions, which, having been asked, will not go away. One returns to the commentaries to ask, How does the kingdom relate to the cross?

---

not one with either sized 'd', I cannot follow him in the rest of his article.

33. Caragounis has written elsewhere on this theme, most notably Caragounis 1989, and a revealing review of G. R. Beasley-Murray's *Jesus and the Kingdom of God* appeared in *Themelios* 14 (1989):69–70. The article in 1992b is the most accessible, however.

34. Caragounis 1992b:422f. Other sayings are capable of meaning that the kingdom 'is arriving/near', rather than – as here – 'has arrived' (for instance, Matt. 3:2; 4:17 = Mark 1:15; 10:7; 12:28 = Luke 11:20). Hence the focus on this verse.

One solution: not linking the kingdom to the cross

One solution is to deny that there is a problem, or at least to relocate the problem elsewhere. For Craig S. Keener, for instance, the issue is to resolve the classic problem that what Jesus appeared to promise did not apparently happen, and he does so by reinforcing the eschatological nature of the kingdom. His commentary on Matthew begins with a number of introductory articles, one of which is on the kingdom:

> It was only natural for Jesus and his followers, once they recognized that Jesus would need to come again to establish his kingdom fully, to recognize that the anticipated kingdom would arrive in two stages corresponding to Jesus' first and second comings . . . [W]e may thus assume that when he announced the kingdom, he undoubtedly announced God's imminent rule in the final sense (rather than simply God's providential rule over creation or over Israel through the law . . .). But in his person, the kingdom was present in a hidden, obscure way, just as the anticipated destiny of a mustard bush was implicitly present in a mustard seed.[35]

That is, of course, true and needs reinforcing. Nevertheless, the precise set of disturbing questions that Caragounis has asked are not addressed.[36] In his comments on these verses, Keener notes, 'If the kingdom has not already "come" in some sense in this verse . . ., it is at least quite imminent,'[37] but it is unclear from the context how the 'quite' in that sentence functions. What is obvious is that there is no mention of the cross, and instead he says that 'the promised time of the kingdom and the Spirit have come on the scene', and 'In establishing the first stage of his kingdom Jesus had *already* defeated the devil.'[38] I confess to finding this opaque. How exactly does the timing work out and connect with the big

---

35. Keener 1999:69.
36. To be clear, I am not expecting that Keener should have responded to Caragounis, but that the approach he takes, which is an excellent example of its type in an admirable commentary, has a blind spot.
37. Keener 1999:364.
38. Keener 1999:364f.

story in Matthew? Rather like an airline passenger who discovers that when her ears 'pop' she can hear sounds that were previously inaudible, so Caragounis's questions make one realize that there are issues to be addressed here, and that the commentators are often unaware of them.

Strikingly, Craig Blomberg is aware of them, but does not tackle them. He claims, quite rightly, that 'Verse 28 is arguably the single most important teaching of Jesus on realized eschatology – the present aspect of the kingdom,' and notices that 'Debate continues on the meaning of *ephthasen* ("has come"), but some sense of *arrival* seems inescapable here.'[39] Unlike Keener, he is even aware that there is a problem, for he refers to Caragounis's ideas in a footnote on this verse. Nevertheless, he seems to do nothing with it.

Caragounis's solution: linking the kingdom to the cross

Caragounis's solution is elegant, if arcane. The Greek word *ephthasen* is in the aorist tense, which is often translated as a past tense – 'has come'. Caragounis argues that there is 'a well-attested but little known and generally misunderstood Greek idiom' by which the aorist tense 'is sometimes used to emphasize the certainty and immediacy of an action that properly belongs in the future by describing it as though it is already here'.[40] In other words, the 'coming of the Kingdom is so imminent that the kingdom of God may be considered as virtually here'.[41] The cross, which will win the defeat over the evil powers, casts its shadow over them in advance.

---

39. Blomberg 1992:202. His solution is, again quite rightly, the classic two-stage arrival of the kingdom, with our living in the overlap of the ages today (73–74). I shall suggest below that this needs some minor fine tuning, but it is not my purpose to disagree with Blomberg's answer to the question of eschatology. It is to note his silence on the question of how this verse relates that problem to the cross. The two commentaries I have quoted are on the Matthean verse, so it is worth noting a similar silence in Lukan commentaries: see, for instance, Green 1997:456f, or Bock 1994:210f.

40. For the lengthy justification see Caragounis 1989.

41. Caragounis 1992b:423.

What is Caragounis attempting to do? In the midst of several
heated debates, three things: (1) to maintain the sense of nearness,
imminence – and threat[42] – of the kingdom, such that Jesus' mere
incarnate presence and miracles do not usher it in; (2) to interpret
the one verse that seems to be counter to that in a different but
academically responsible way; and (3) to tie the imminence of the
kingdom not to some deferred parousia but to the victory won by
the Son of Man on the cross, which will then result in that
deferred parousia. Everything then hangs on point 2: can he convincingly show that the aorist can have the sense of 'an advance,
but not quite the presence of the kingdom of God'?

I think he can, but it may not be necessary to argue the case for
'a well-attested but little known and generally misunderstood
Greek idiom'. The fault lies rather with the habitual understanding
that the aorist is normally a past 'once-and-for-all' tense, and that
the exceptions to that have to be argued for.[43] It is now common
currency in Greek grammar textbooks to deny any specific 'past'
meaning to the aorist. David Black writes:

> Aoristic aspect was used when the Greek writer didn't want you to pay
> any attention to the duration or completion of the action. Think of it as
> a snapshot: 'Jesus *wept*', 'Christ *died* for our sins', 'God so *loved* the
> world', and so on . . . Thus . . . (Rom 5:14) covers the whole period from
> Adam to Moses in which death 'reigned'; . . . (Heb 11:23) covers a
> period of three months in which Moses 'was hidden'; . . . (John 2:20)
> covers a period of forty-six years during which the temple 'was built';
> and . . . (Matt 28:19) covers the entire church age in which Christians are
> to 'make disciples'. So never jump to the conclusion that aoristic aspect
> is instantaneous. The action *may* be instantaneous, but only the context
> or the meaning of the verb can tell you that . . . [A]oristic aspect is
> about as mundane a category as you can find. And it never means 'once

---

42. The threat is contained in the phrase 'upon you'.

43. Those of us who learned our Greek from John Wenham's textbook
    (1965) will perhaps fall prey to this error. It is perhaps Wenham's use of
    the term 'punctiliar' which is most unhelpful, because it seems to imply
    that a finished event is brief.

and for all', no matter who tells you that it does. As someone has put it, 'Its special meaning is that it does not have a special meaning.' Period.[44]

Given that the aorist has more breadth to its meaning than we might think, is there New Testament warrant for using it for a future event which is so certain that we can talk of it as if it were already present? Consider these three verses:

> Therefore I tell you, whatever you ask in prayer, believe that *you have received it*, and it will be yours (Mark 11:24; my italics).

> When he had gone out, Jesus said, 'Now *is* the Son of Man *glorified*, and God *is glorified* in him' (John 13:31; my italics).

> And those whom he predestined he also called, and those whom he called he also justified, and those whom he justified *he* also *glorified* (Romans 8:30; my italics).[45]

All three are clear examples, to my mind, that the aorist may well be used of a future event that is so certain that it can be talked of as a present reality. Returning to Matthew 12:28, then, there is solid ground for agreeing with Caragounis that the aorist may have the sense he suggests here, and that once we have taken off our blinkers on the breadth of meaning of the aorist, the question is whether it does mean that. And that can be given only by the context.

Context: Son of Man and the kingdom
The immediate debate is over the effectiveness and meaning of Jesus' exorcisms, but the broader background lies in the discussions over who Jesus is:[46] whether he is indeed the 'Servant' that Isaiah predicted (Matt. 12:18; Isa. 42:10–13), or the 'Son of

----

44. Black 1998:96f. A more scholarly approach is taken in Wallace 1996a:554–565, from which the following examples are taken.
45. Wallace 1996:564.
46. Matt. 8:20; 9:6; 10:23; 11:19; 12:8, 32, 40; 13:37, 41; 16:13, 27f; 17:9, 12, 22; 19:28; 20:18, 28; 24:27, 30, 37, 39, 44; 25:31; 26:2, 24, 45, 64.

Man' that Daniel foretold (Matt. 12:32; Dan. 7).

Within Matthew's references to Son of Man, the central idea is one that he has clearly derived from Daniel, that the Son of Man will rule over a kingdom (Dan. 7:14), and that the kingdom is a rival – even a threat – to the established world orders. Thus even though the title 'Son of Man' is not identified with it, the Great Commission in chapter 28 is based on the authority that the crucified and risen Jesus has been given, echoing Daniel 7. Caragounis's insight on Matthew 12 is that 'the Son of Man's attacks on the kingdom of evil, ought not to be construed in terms of the Hellenistic or Jewish exorcist's activity but rather be connected with the Son of Man's mission . . ., otherwise the link between the kingdom of God and the cross becomes illegitimately obscured'.[47] Certainly, the weight of references to the Son of Man in Matthew have as their centre that 'the Son of Man came not to be served but to serve, and to give his life as a ransom for many' (20:28). Luke does not have that phrase, but equally ties the title in with the idea of the Son of Man's ruling and judging beyond his death and resurrection, and ties the title to one of his major themes, 'For the Son of Man came to seek and to save the lost' (19:10).[48]

There is, then, a close connection between the title 'Son of Man', the kingdom he will win and rule over and the cross.

Context: servant and the kingdom

The title 'servant' is much rarer in the Gospels, although Matthew has highlighted its significance by placement of the Isaiah quotation.[49] The other occurrence of the title in his Gospel is significant in view of what has just been seen:

> Then the mother of the sons of Zebedee came up to him with her sons, and kneeling before him she asked him for something. And he said to her,

---

47. Caragounis 1992b:425. His point here refers particularly to Mark 10:45 – for clarity I have used the Matthean parallel.
48. Luke 5:24; 6:5, 22; 7:34; 9:22, 26, 44, 58; 11:30; 12:8, 10, 40; 17:22, 24, 26, 30; 18:8, 31; 19:10; 21:27, 36; 22:22, 48, 69; 24:7.
49. Luke does not use the Isaiah quotation.

'What do you want?' She said to him, 'Say that these two sons of mine are to sit, one at your right hand and one at your left, in your kingdom.' Jesus answered, 'You do not know what you are asking. Are you able to drink the cup that I am to drink?' They said to him, 'We are able.' He said to them, 'You will drink my cup, but to sit at my right hand and at my left is not mine to grant, but it is for those for whom it has been prepared by my Father.' And when the ten heard it, they were indignant at the two brothers. But Jesus called them to him and said, 'You know that the rulers of the Gentiles lord it over them, and their great ones exercise authority over them. It shall not be so among you. But whoever would be great among you must be your servant and whoever would be first among you must be your slave, even as the Son of Man came not to be served but to serve, and to give his life as a ransom for many.'

And as they went out of Jericho, a great crowd followed him. And behold, there were two blind men sitting by the roadside, and when they heard that Jesus was passing by, they cried out, 'Lord, have mercy on us, Son of David!' The crowd rebuked them, telling them to be silent, but they cried out all the more, 'Lord, have mercy on us, Son of David!' And stopping, Jesus called them and said, 'What do you want me to do for you?' They said to him, 'Lord, let our eyes be opened.' And Jesus in pity touched their eyes, and immediately they recovered their sight and followed him (20:20–34).

Three points are worth observing here: (1) the title 'Servant' occurs again in close proximity to the title 'Son of Man'; (2) it does so in a section that is unambiguously about Jesus' death, and where the title 'Son of Man' is used in that context; (3) this is a context where a number of other 'ruler' titles are being similarly aligned with the cross: Son of David, Lord and (implied in the title 'Father') Son of God.

Once again, we are forced by the dynamic of the narrative theology to interpret our themes of the kingdom in terms of the victory won by the cross.

The kingdom in the Old Testament

In one sense, we should have begun with the Old Testament material on the kingdom, but in another sense we have already seen what we need. Here we can simply summarize the major patterns that have already been drawn on.

Although it is well known, it is still striking that the phrases 'The kingdom of God' or 'the kingdom of heaven' are themselves absent from the Old Testament,[50] but that is only a minor verbal point when we consider the wealth of material on God's rightful lordship of his world as his creation.[51] There are the repeated assertions that the Lord has a kingdom,[52] a throne,[53] a sceptre,[54] a footstool,[55] and so on, and many occurrences of the idea that he is a king.[56] The very title 'Lord' is a royal one. That relation is expressed in a series of concentric circles, moving inward from the whole of creation, through humankind, to Israel, and then to the human king himself.[57] Just as Adam functioned as God's vice-gerent for the whole of creation, so David and his successors function as God's vice-gerents in Israel.[58] God's kingly rule is expressed uniquely but not exhaustively through the rule of the kings from Jerusalem.

More accurately, his is a *rebelled-against* lordship, archetypically from the rebellion in the garden. The Lord–subject relation is

---

50. Wisdom 1:10 contains the words.

51. Pss. 47:7–8; 103:19; Dan. 4:17, 34–35.

52. E.g. 1 Chron. 17:14; 28:5; Pss. 103:19; 145:11.

53. E.g. Pss. 9:4; 45:6; 47:8; Isa. 6:1; Ezek. 1:26.

54. Pss. 45:6; 60:7; 110:2.

55. 1 Chron. 28:2; Pss. 99:5; 110:1; 132:7; Isa. 66:1.

56. E.g. Deut. 9:26; 1 Sam. 12:12; Pss. 24:10; 29:10.

57. The idea of a growing reign of God from creation onwards is worked out in Beale 2004.

58. Presumably, Adam's successors would have functioned in this way, too. Jesus is therefore appropriately both Son of David and Son of Man/Adam in this regard. To labour a point, a vice-*regent* is a substitute for an absent monarch, so Lord Curzon was a substitute for Queen Victoria in India from 1898 to 1905; but a vice-*gerent* has a delegated royal authority in the presence of a monarch (like Solomon who was anointed king during his father's lifetime in 1 Kgs 1:28–53). This allows us to see how Jesus can claim to be the King, and yet for the kingdom to be God's kingdom, because his authority is exercised under the Father's rule.

shown in God's question 'Have you eaten of the tree of which I *commanded* you not to eat?' (Gen. 3:11; my italics). Throughout Israel's history, the downturns in her relationship are described in similar Lord–subject terms as rebellion,[59] treason[60] or disobedience.[61] Yet the Bible is not a picture of an ongoing tolerated rebellion but the implementation of a saving covenantal lordship. The day will dawn when God will become king,[62] by replacing and punishing those who have usurped his rule, whether they be foreign rulers[63] or Israelite pretenders,[64] and establishing his own monarchy of forgiven and obedient ex-rebels.[65] Psalm 2 is a clear example.

> Why do the nations rage
>   and the peoples plot in vain?
> The kings of the earth set themselves,
>   and the rulers take counsel together,
>   against the LORD and against his anointed, saying,
> 'Let us burst their bonds apart
>   and cast away their cords from us.'
>
> He who sits in the heavens laughs;
>   the Lord holds them in derision.
> Then he will speak to them in his wrath,
>   and terrify them in his fury, saying,

---

59. Exod. 23:21; 34:7; Lev. 16:16, 21; Num. 14:9, 18; 20:10; Deut. 13:5; 31:27; Josh. 1:18; 22:16, 18f, 22, 29; 24:19; 1 Sam. 12:14f; 15:23; 12:19; 16:20; 2 Kgs 8:22; 2 Chron. 10:19; 21:10; Neh. 9:17; Job 24:13; 34:37; Ps. 106:43; Prov. 17:11; Isa. 1:5, 20, 23, 28; 24:20; 46:8; 48:8; 57:4; 58:1; 59:13; Jer. 5:6; 6:28; 28:16; 29:32; 33:8; Ezek. 2:8; 20:38; 21:24; Hos. 5:2.

60. Lev. 26:40; Isa. 21:2; 24:16; 33:1; 59:13.

61. Num. 14:22, 41; 27:14; Deut. 11:28; Josh. 22:22; Judg. 2:2; 2 Chron. 24:20; Neh. 9:26, 29; Isa. 24:5; Jer. 42:13; 43:4, 7; Ezek. 33:12.

62. Isa. 52:7–10; Ezek. 34:11–24; Mic. 4:7; Zech. 14:9.

63. Ezek. 34:27–28; 1 Chron. 17:9.

64. Ezek. 34:10.

65. Isa. 2:1–5; 11:1–9; Mic. 4:1–8; Ezek. 34:11–31; 37:21–24; Dan 7:27; Zech. 9:9–10.

'As for me, I have set my King
  on Zion, my holy hill.'

I will tell of the decree:
  The LORD said to me, 'You are my Son;
  today I have begotten you.
Ask of me, and I will make the nations your heritage,
  and the ends of the earth your possession.
You shall break them with a rod of iron
  and dash them in pieces like a potter's vessel.'

Now therefore, O kings, be wise;
  be warned, O rulers of the earth.
Serve the LORD with fear,
  and rejoice with trembling.
Kiss the Son, lest he be angry, and you perish in the way,
  for his wrath is quickly kindled.
  Blessed are all who take their refuge in him.

Jesus' claim to be the Son of David would be enough, then, to tap into this line of the promise of a rejuvenated, global Davidic monarchy.[66] We would expect his rule to be expressed in a growing set of concentric circles, spreading from Jerusalem to encompass the entire cosmos as he increasingly exercises his rule over a growing band of delighted subjects and a growing crowd of defeated enemies, until his final and decisive conquest.

But it is clear from his frequent exposition of the psalms in particular that Jesus identified with another motif, too, that of the suffering and vindicated King. A number of psalms have something like the following pattern.[67]

---

66. Isa. 9:7, 11:1–15; Ezek. 34:23.
67. This table is drawn from comparing Pss. 2–11 (?12), 13 (?14–15), 16–18, 20–28, 30–31 (?33), 34–35, 38–41 (?42–43), 44–45, 49, 52, 54–57, 59, 63 (?66), 67–70, 72 (?74), 75 (?79), 80 (?83), 84, 86, 88–89, 92 (?94), 102–103 (?107), 109–110 (?112), 115–116, 118 (?119), 121, 132–133, 138, 142–143, 145, 148. That is a minimum of sixty-eight psalms, and a maximum of eighty-two.

The Davidic King,
God's Son,
Is unjustly opposed
By his enemies
Who are also God's enemies.
He is brought to a state of scorn, pain and rejection
Which is identified with death.
God answers the king's prayer for rescue
Because of his covenant,
And so there is life beyond the peril
Which will be eternal
With an eternal throne for this King.
This victory causes God's people to praise
At a victory banquet
In the sight of the nations
Who are either drawn to worship and obey
Or to be judged and condemned.

Some of those psalms explore only part of this journey, or even one moment, but they have sufficiently frequent quotation in the New Testament, along the lines of this shape as an explanation for Jesus' ministry in its widest compass, that they clearly are an essential element of Jesus' self-understanding of himself as King.

The third element we have also noted is the identification of the Son of Man with the one who receives and rules over a future, restored kingdom. Daniel 7, and especially verse 14, is critical for the identification, but it is not often noted that this is entirely of a piece with the notion of a renewed Davidic monarch that will impact the whole of creation. Daniel is not eccentric, therefore, in having this motif, nor is Jesus plucking an odd phrase from one obscure passage when he uses it.

Implications

Let me draw two brief pastoral implications from what we have seen, and begin to address the questions we began with. Is there a different way of presenting the gospel, which talks of the kingdom rather than the cross?

Evangelicals and an inaugurated eschatology
In the article mentioned above, Caragounis argues that if the terms *kingdom, eternal life* and so on are parallel terms, then we must see the cross as inaugurating the kingdom.[68] This sounds unexceptional until we realize that if kingdom and cross are disconnected, then there is a possibility (taken by some) that the kingdom is inaugurated by Jesus' incarnation, not by the cross, and that it is his presence rather than his cross-work which should be announced.[69] This would give, not just a different language set to describe the

---

68. Caragounis 1992b.

69. On the danger of an inadequate theology of the incarnation see the papers from a previous Oak Hill School of Theology (Peterson 2003), especially chs. 1, 2 and 4.

gospel, but a different content. I have argued, following Caragounis, that the reverse is the case.

If the cross inaugurates the kingdom, then we stand today in an inaugurated kingdom. Again, this is widely agreed territory, so let me be more specific. Evangelicals, especially conservative evangelicals, often criticize those who have what might be termed an overinaugurated view of the kingdom.[70] That is, those who trivialize, explain away, discount or even deny the presence of sin, sickness and other consequences of the fall in the life of the contemporary believer. Quite rightly, we want a more thoughtful view, which is frequently explained as the difference between 'now' and 'not yet'. True, different people put subtly different content in those two boxes, but the tension between 'now' and 'not yet' is a frequently encountered explanation.

However, I want to suggest that the model slightly misrepresents the New Testament material, because it could be seen to imply that there is 'now' not much difference between a Christian and a non-Christian except that we have the intangibles of faith, forgiveness and the dowry-gift of the Spirit, and that everything really substantial is 'not yet'. But if the cross has inaugurated the kingdom, then we should rather think that those three things are wonderful, life-changing gifts, along with many other things God provides, and it is unhelpful to downplay the differences they make. It might be merely a matter of presentation, but we could be understood to be offering an 'underrealized' eschatology in which, in effect, all that has happened is that we believe several truths that we used not to believe, and hope for various events that used to seem nonsense. That would leave no room at all for any change of life beyond a change of mind.

Perhaps it would be pastorally more helpful to redraw our normal two columns as three: the 'no longer', the 'now' and the 'not yet', which would give a rationale and motivation for grateful, repentant and life-transforming Christian change based on what

---

70. I use 'overinaugurated' rather than the more common 'overrealized' because the latter has particular technical resonances with the work of C. H. Dodd, which muddies the waters of the point I am trying to make.

has been achieved by the cross, without in any way having to misappropriate those wonders that are 'not yet' ours. A Christian would then be assured that he is 'no longer' under God's condemnation, is 'not yet' sinless, and is therefore required 'now' to struggle with sin as a defeated enemy. *Inauguration* by the cross places us in the kingdom of God's victory; inauguration *by the cross* reminds us of the pattern of discipleship to which the victorious King calls us.

So a Christian who struggles with, say, alcohol abuse is given three resources: a forgiveness which has been won already with a guarantee that he is '*no longer* . . . enslaved to sin*' (Rom. 6:6) and that if he does sin he can say 'it is *no longer* I who do it, but sin that dwells within me' (Rom. 7:20); a promise of a sin-free eternity which will one day be his, but 'At present, we do *not yet* see everything in subjection to him' (Christ) (Heb. 2:8); and the constant presence of the Holy Spirit to challenge and comfort him into the likeness of Christ by all the aspects of his work, because '*now* we are released from the law, having died to that which held us captive, so that we serve not under the old written code but in the new life of the Spirit' (Rom. 7:6). Those three elements would be the informing theology to explain why he must 'not get drunk with wine, for that is debauchery, but be filled with the Spirit' (Eph. 5:18). We must not downplay the impact of reassuring people not only of what they 'now' have, and what is 'not yet' theirs, though it will be, but critically, of what is 'no longer' true about them, because of their entry into the kingdom through the cross.

The gospel, the kingdom and evangelism
We have seen that in the Synoptics and Acts, 'the gospel' and 'the kingdom' are fundamentally related. They are not different messages, as some old-school liberals might once have tried to have us believe.[71] But nor is it adequate to see them as two different ways

---

71. From a previous generation, then, it is worth recalling the clarifying work of Reginald H. Fuller in his response to, and thorough critique of, Rudolf Bultmann over the place of the cross in the ministry of Jesus. 'To interpret Jesus as an eschatological prophet who simply announced the impending advent of the eschatological Reign of God, challenged men to

of describing the same reality but with different vocabularies, which different people might find easier or harder to accept. That thought might seem on the surface to be evangelistically useful, because we could talk using different kinds of language to different groups of people, according to their needs and pastoral appropriateness, but it is actually flawed. If I could explain the gospel to people, fully and without distortion, and do so without leading them to expect forgiveness for sin on the basis of the cross (for instance), then what I have produced is not alternative language but an alternative gospel, because the substance has changed.

Put simply, the gospel of the kingdom as we find it in Acts is the announcement of forgiveness and the gift of the Spirit that flow necessarily from the throne of the crucified and risen Saviour-King. We saw above that the appropriate response to hearing the gospel is repentance and faith. To ask people to repent and believe when they have heard a message that does not focus on the death and resurrection of Jesus actually asks for a different reason for repentance and a different message to believe. Do they, then, receive forgiveness and the gift of the Spirit? Since we have seen that talking about the kingdom *requires* us to talk about the cross, any such detachment must be theologically, and spiritually, disastrous.

There are many audiences, but only one gospel. To present that one gospel under the language of the kingdom is not necessarily to alter it. But if we use it because we think someone is more likely to respond to the language of the kingdom than that of, say, justification or forgiveness, and that is precisely because we wrongly think the kingdom does not operate in that theological field, then we have altered it by distorting the cross-work of the king.

© Chris Green, 2006.

---

preparatory decision in the face of that impending event, and left it at that, is an entirely inadequate reconstructing of the history of Jesus of Nazareth ... Jesus has been sent not only to announce the coming Reign of God, but to perform the decisive event through which God will inaugurate that Reign' (Fuller 1967:77).

5. THE GOSPEL OF PAUL AND THE GOSPEL OF THE KINGDOM

Simon Gathercole

Introduction

The New Testament authors were united in their understanding of the gospel both in their preaching ministries and in their literary legacy (i.e. the New Testament documents). The first four books of the New Testament were not merely regarded as 'The Four Gospels', but as works attesting to the *one* gospel, that according to Matthew, Mark, Luke and John.[1] These Gospels are, furthermore, not independent of one another; rather, Mark's Gospel was the basis of Matthew and Luke. Luke perhaps used Matthew's Gospel,[2]

---

1. Hengel 1984 makes a number of important points on this matter. He notes the prevalence of references to 'the gospel' in the second century, even when the Gospel accounts are meant (see his p. 11 for some of the papyrological evidence, and p. 20 for literary indications). He notes that, to his knowledge, the plural *euangelia* occurs only twice prior to Irenaeus (p. 14).

2. For the best recent defence of this proposal, and concomitant opposition

and John may well have presumed the circulation of Mark's Gospel.[3]

Nor did the process of the formation of the Gospels take place in isolation from that of the epistles. The linguistic and theological commonalities between the Johannine epistles and the Gospel of John have been widely recognized. There is a very strong probability that Paul was the mentor of Luke, the author of Luke-Acts.[4] Less certain, but still quite plausible, is the case that has perennially been made for Mark's Gospel as a product of the Pauline school.[5] So not only do some of the Gospels build on others, but some of them also emerged from the same circles that also produced the epistles as well – another reason why we should not be surprised to find theological harmony.[6]

The concern in this chapter is with the extent to which Paul's gospel is the same as, or represents a radical departure from, that of the Gospel writers and the other apostles. Relevant here is one of the most striking pieces of evidence for the harmony within the apostolic preaching, a very brief comment by Paul after his own summary of the gospel and list of the witnesses to the resurrection in 1 Corinthians 15:

> But by the grace of God I am what I am, and his grace towards me was not in vain. On the contrary, I worked harder than any of them, though it was not I, but the grace of God that is with me. *Whether then it was I or they, so we preach and so you believed* (1 Cor. 15:10–11, my italics).

So Paul affirms that all the people he has just mentioned as witnesses of the risen Jesus – he himself, Peter, the rest of the Twelve, and James the brother of the Lord – are all in exactly the

---

to the Q hypothesis, see Goodacre 2001.

3. See R. J. Bauckham, 'John for Readers of Mark', in Bauckham 1998:147–171.

4. On the issues here see Thornton 1991.

5. Most recently, Joel Marcus has evaluated some of the most important proponents and opponents of this hypothesis in the twentieth century (Marcus 2000).

6. 2 Pet. 3:15–16 also refers to 'all' the letters of Paul.

same evangelistic boat: they have all believed the same gospel and preach that same gospel.[7]

One of the main challenges to this view came in the nineteenth century from the Tübingen school, and still persists into the present. The argument goes – drawing on Galatians 2 in particular – that Paul was in fact extremely isolated in advocating a Law-free gospel and a radical integration of Jew and Gentile.[8] The problem with this line, however, is that Paul, Peter and James were preaching the same gospel not only in the mid-50s when Paul wrote 1 Corinthians 15 but also in the late 40s at the time (probably) of the Antioch incident and the composition of Galatians.[9] In Galatians 2, Paul does not fault Peter's theological understanding of the gospel, but rather whether he is living according to it at Antioch. Previously, in Galatians 2:1–10, there had been a remarkable display of unity among Paul, Peter, James and John, in opposition to 'those of the circumcision'.[10] The 'pillars' of the Jerusalem church had not insisted on Titus, Paul's companion, being circumcised; on the contrary, they seem to have shared full fellowship with him in Galatians 2:1–10. The same leaders of the Jerusalem church also offered Paul and Barnabas the right hand of fellowship for the Gentile mission.[11]

---

7. On the importance of this often neglected statement, see Hengel and Schwemer 1997.

8. See the bibliography and description of the views of Baur, Schweitzer and Barrett in Gathercole 2005:309–310.

9. These dates remain provisional, of course, and nothing of substance depends on them for the main burden of the present argument.

10. See the argument in Gathercole 2005:309–327.

11. This is not to deny that very early on there were heretics in the church, whether of a Law-enforcing or proto-gnosticizing kind. In the first category, we obviously have the target of Paul's opposition in Galatians, which he denounces as preaching another gospel. On the other hand, there are those who go even further than Eph. 2 in the overrealization of eschatology: Hymenaeus and Philetus in 2 Tim. 2:17–18 consider that the resurrection has already happened. So it is not the point here to argue that the gospel remained uncontaminated throughout the apostolic period.

This chapter aims to build on these historical points by identifying the specific ways in which Paul's gospel can be seen to have the same content at its centre as the gospel in the Gospels. The chapter, then, will consist of two parts, the first on Paul, and the second offering some comparisons with the Gospels. Within each of these parts, there will be examination of the three core elements of the gospel as God's account of his saving activity (1) in Jesus the Messiah, in which, by Jesus' death and resurrection he (2) atones for sin and (3) brings new creation.

The Pauline gospel

There are two bodies of texts which are most useful for identifying the content of Paul's gospel. The first is the sermons of Paul in Acts, which – if the point above about Luke as witness of Paul's ministry is correct – should be given much more credence than is usually allowed. However, Acts is covered by Chris Green elsewhere in this book, and my brief is to explore the second: the summary statements and other comments in the epistles themselves.

As has already been mentioned, the focus here will be on the three aspects of the gospel message that are central in Paul (which also emerge in the Gospel narratives). These consist of (1) who Jesus is, with particular reference to his identity as royal Messiah and son of God; (2) his work of atonement and justification accomplished in the cross and resurrection, and (3) Jesus' work of new creation and of rescue from the power of sin. These three elements are the core of the *euangelion* according to Paul.

The gospel of who Jesus is: Romans 1:3–4
The gospel according to Paul is simultaneously an affirmation of *who* Jesus is as well as of *what* he has done. This is reflected in the fact that much New Testament scholarship nowadays refuses to

---

But it is to deny that a pluralistic heterodoxy *preceded* an apostolic orthodoxy, an orthodoxy that emerged only later with the triumph of conformity over heresy.

draw a sharp distinction between Christology and soteriology.
Here, however, we shall do so – at least for heuristic purposes –
and deal first with Jesus' identity by focusing on Romans 1:3–4:

> Paul, a servant of Christ Jesus, called to be an apostle, set apart for the
> gospel of God, which he promised beforehand through his prophets in
> the holy Scriptures, concerning his Son, who was descended from David
> according to the flesh, and was declared to be the Son of God in power
> according to the Spirit of holiness by his resurrection from the dead,
> Jesus Christ our Lord (Rom. 1:1–4).

In this statement from Paul, then, Jesus is Son of God twice over.
He is 'from the seed of David' by being a member of Joseph's
family, so possessing the Davidic lineage that is a minimal requirement for a messianic claim. 'Son of God' can simply be understood
in this sense – that just as God could call David his son in Psalm 2,
so David's descendant in 2 Samuel 7 was entitled to the same desig-
nation. Paul's Christology, however, is not merely confined to this
Davidic understanding of Jesus' divine sonship. Paul understands
Jesus as pre-existent Son of God, as well as powerfully *post*-existent.
This is the key point of verse 4, that in the resurrection Jesus was
declared Son of God in power and appointed to his position at the
right hand of God, as Lord (Col. 3:1; cf. Rom. 8:3). Central to both
Davidic descent according to the flesh and his appointment *in power*
is that they each underscore Jesus' *royal* status, his lordship and reign
over the whole world. Colossians 1:15–20 is a majestic statement of
this, portraying the full extent of Jesus' dominion over heaven and
earth and everything in them. So the *identity* of Jesus is the first
central aspect of Paul's gospel.

Christ's death and resurrection for sins and justification
When it comes to the Gospels' account of what Jesus has *done*, we
are on fairly safe ground in going to 1 Corinthians 15. This is
because the first few verses make it explicit that Paul is here
recounting the gospel that he preached in Corinth:

> Now I would remind you, brothers, of the gospel I preached to you,
> which you received, in which you stand, [2] and by which you are being

saved, if you hold fast to the word I preached to you – unless you believed in vain.

For I delivered to you as of first importance what I also received (1 Cor. 15:1–3a).

So Paul here is explicitly recounting the gospel, as well as what he regards as being 'of first importance'.[12] As a result, it is difficult to see why the most recent book on Paul's gospel, by Douglas Campbell, pays so little attention to 1 Corinthians 15.[13] The chapter receives only a few mentions in passing and in footnotes, and Campbell's book is much more concerned with discovering which of Romans 1 – 4, or 5 – 8 or 9 – 11 is the true exposition of the gospel. On the other hand, 1 Corinthians 15 can sometimes be neglected by British evangelicals as well, and simply be used in 'evidence for the resurrection' talks.

On another level, the account in 1 Corinthians 15 calls into question the view that the single centre of the gospel is the lordship of Jesus.[14] This is of course essential to the gospel, but it is not sufficient as an account. As 1 Corinthians 15 shows, the explication of the events by which this has taken place (the death and resurrection of Jesus) are integral, indeed central, to the proclamation of the gospel.[15]

---

12. Thiselton notes that *en prōtois* is strictly speaking to be understood logically rather than temporally here, while allowing for some ambiguity (Thiselton 2000:1186).

13. Campbell 2005.

14. See e.g. Wright 1997:114. Or as he eloquently puts it elsewhere, 'The Gospel is the announcement that Jesus is Lord – Lord of the world, Lord of the cosmos, Lord of the earth, of the ozone layer, of whales and waterfalls, of trees and tortoises' (1997:154–155).

15. Indeed, Wright – while maintaining an insistence on defining the gospel as the proclamation of the lordship of Jesus – would probably affirm this; his polemic against an identification of the gospel *tout simple* with a doctrine of justification that is detached from the proclamation of the lordship of Christ is probably what gives rise to his somewhat one-sided formulation in the places noted above.

Another issue which 1 Corinthians 15 addresses, albeit indirectly, is whether the gospel can be written down and defined, or whether it exists in proclamation only or requires reinterpretation in every generation. To answer this, it is clear that the gospel has both permanent relevance and changeless content. So Paul pronounces the divine curse on anyone who tells the Galatians anything different from what they originally heard. In chapter 15 here, he similarly reminds the Corinthians of the gospel he preached to them, and rehearses its content in written form. The gospel is not the events themselves, but the report of the events. It has cognitive content, and as such cannot only be told (1 Thess. 2:2) and preached (e.g. 1 Cor. 9:16), but can also be defended and safeguarded (Phil. 1:7; 2 Tim. 1:13–14).

As to what it says the gospel is, we turn to verses 3–8:

> For I delivered to you as of first importance what I also received: that Christ died for our sins in accordance with the Scriptures, that he was buried, that he was raised on the third day in accordance with the Scriptures, and that he appeared to Cephas, then to the twelve. Then he appeared to more than five hundred brothers at one time, most of whom are still alive, though some have fallen asleep. Then he appeared to James, then to all the apostles. Last of all, as to one untimely born, he appeared also to me (1 Cor. 15:3–8).

The language used here in connection with the death of Christ taps into the common formula of Christ 'dying for', as in:

> Christ died for the ungodly (Rom. 5:6).

> Christ died for us (Rom. 5:8).

> who . . . gave himself for me (Gal. 2:20).

> who gave himself as a ransom for all (1 Tim. 2:6).

Closest, however, is the parallel in Galatians 1:4, 'who gave himself for our sins', where the reference is not only to dying *for us*, but specifically *for our sins*. As has been argued elsewhere, the interchangeability of the statements of Christ's death 'for us' and the language of his death 'for our sins' points strongly in a substitutionary direction.[16] This is also present in 1 Peter: 'For Christ also suffered once *for sins, the righteous for the unrighteous*' (1 Pet. 3:18, my italics; cf. 2:24). This relation taps into the Old Testament tradition of death as the penalty for sin that begins in Genesis 2 – 3 and permeates the whole canon thereafter.

In Genesis, God spells out to Adam and Eve that if they disobey his command, they will surely die (Gen. 2:17). When they do disobey, they lose their capacity to live forever by being prohibited access to the tree of life. So disobedience leads to the divine punishment of death. Similarly, in the Law, God presents Israel with a choice of life or death (Deut. 30:17–20). Life comes from obedience to the commandments (Lev. 18:5 etc.), and death and destruction are the divine penalties for forsaking Torah (e.g. Deut. 28:20–24).

The difference between Paul and the majority of the Old Testament, however, is that in Christ's death, it is one who has never sinned who suffers the consequences of it. This does not really mean 'as a consequence of sins' in the sense that Jesus' death is the result of the sin-ridden judicial process as narrated in the trial narratives in the Gospels, though this is not far from Paul's mind.[17] Rather, the consequence of transgression which we saw spelt out in Genesis and Deuteronomy above (i.e. death) is borne by Jesus. In fact, the Pauline statements above refer specifically to Christ's bearing the punishment, and not strictly speaking to his bearing sin(s), though that is undoubtedly true.[18] Paul does speak, however, of Jesus hyperbolically *becoming* the sin (2 Cor. 5:21) just as he talks of him becoming the punishment, or curse, as well (Gal. 3:13). Indeed, God's condemnation of sin in the flesh presumes Jesus' bearing of sin in his flesh (Rom. 8:3).

In Paul's argument in Romans 1 – 3, the implication of this is spelt out in some detail as *justification*. Romans 3:21–26 provides both a longer version of the 'death for sin' formula mentioned above, and its relation to justification. In brief, while God had not

---

16. Gathercole 2003:161–162.

17. Note the ambiguity of the *paredothē* in Rom. 4:25.

18. As in, say, 1 Pet. 2:24: 'He himself bore our sins in his body on the tree . . .'

punished sin in full prior to the coming of Christ, in the cross, that full measure of retribution is exacted on the cross. And so this action in Christ simultaneously demonstrates God's justice (in that he does not let sin go unpunished), as well as his righteous salvation. He is both just, and the justifier.[19] It is this act of God as the one who pronounces people righteous that occupies Paul's argument for the rest of chapter 3 and the whole of chapter 4. That Romans 3:21–26 is also an exposition of the gospel is clear from the connection to Romans 1:16–17. The gospel is the place where 'the righteousness of God is revealed', according to 1:16–17, and Rom. 3:21–26 begins with the almost identical language of the righteousness of God being made manifest in the events described there.

In 1 Corinthians 15 and Romans 3, we have in this deliberate articulation by Paul of his gospel an explicit statement of Christ's atoning work. As a result, I find it hard to fathom how Campbell can argue that 'the atoning work of the cross' is present only in a 'marginal role' here.[20] The importance of the atonement–justification sequence in Paul's thought can be seen in his exploration of the implications of justification in Romans 5:1–11: peace with God, access to him, and the boast in God through Christ.

Finally, as far as justification is concerned, it is important to note that for Paul the resurrection also is related to justification: 'who was delivered up for our trespasses and raised for our justification' (Rom. 4:25). Paul draws no hard distinction between justification and new life: just as the analogy is drawn between the justification of the ungodly and the creation of life from non-life in Romans 4, so in Romans 5:18 he can say that the coming of Christ brings to all *dikaiōsin zōēs*, literally, 'justification of life'. But we need to expand the discussion of resurrection more widely at this point.

New creation, and rescue from the dominion of sin

The resurrection is no mere afterthought in Paul's gospel, and nowhere is this clearer than in 1 Corinthians 15. The gospel is an account of both Jesus' death and resurrection indivisibly, as is also

---

19. For a detailed treatment of these verses see Gathercole 2004a:177–181.
20. Campbell 2005:198 and n. 43.

implied in Paul's presupposition that as Christians 'we believe that Jesus died and rose again' (1 Thess. 4:14). One factor implicit here is that the portrayal of the death and resurrection of Christ clarifies the relation of the gospel to history, time and space. The gospel is in no way detached from history – God's saving action does not take place in some Gnostic other-worldly sphere, but in the real world; specifically, in the flesh of Christ: as noted already, Romans 8:3 talks about sin being punished on the cross in Christ's flesh. And Christ really was raised bodily, not merely as an apparition.[21] However, the key point of the resurrection for Paul is that Christ's new life means our new life, both at the eschaton when we receive new bodies, but also in the present.

One point on which Paul still agreed with his Pharisaic contemporaries is in the view that all people – both righteous and wicked alike – would be raised from the dead by God at the judgment. Based on Daniel 12, the idea was common in early Judaism and in the New Testament that there would be a 'general resurrection' on the last day. To quote a Pauline example:

If the Spirit of him who raised Jesus from the dead dwells in you, he who raised Christ Jesus from the dead will also give life to your mortal bodies through his Spirit who dwells in you (Rom. 8:11).

Here Paul is about to launch into the exposition in Romans 8:18–27 of 'the glory that is to be revealed in us' (8:18). This will come when the whole of creation is set free from decay, and – as in 1 Corinthians 15 – our bodies are transformed into a glorious state (Rom. 8:21, 23).

Additionally, however, Paul articulates a position that is less common in earliest Christianity; namely, that resurrection life is also a present reality:

God . . . made us alive together with Christ . . . and raised us up with him and seated us with him in the heavenly places in Christ Jesus, so that in the coming ages he might show the immeasurable riches of his grace in kindness towards us in Christ Jesus (Eph. 2:4–7).

---

21. See the discussions of this issue throughout Wright 2003.

So here, in this radical statement of the present condition that Christians inhabit, we are already resurrected with Christ, and no longer live in the mundane reality of the old age, but in the heavenly sphere.

However, it is not only in the resurrection that this new life and new realm are created. Christ also destroys *in the cross* the powers of sin and death:

> and he died for all, that those who live might no longer live for themselves but for him who for their sake died and was raised (2 Cor. 5:15).

> Grace to you and peace from God our Father and the Lord Jesus Christ, who gave himself for our sins to deliver us from the present evil age, according to the will of our God and Father (Gal. 1:3–4).

> But far be it from me to boast except in the cross of our Lord Jesus Christ, by which the world has been crucified to me, and I to the world. For neither circumcision counts for anything, nor uncircumcision, but a new creation (Gal. 6:14–15).

Christ died 'for all' not only to atone for individuals' transgressions, but also to pronounce destruction on the old world and create a new one. As those who have been delivered from the previous age that was controlled by Satan, Christians now live for Christ. The most substantial exposition of this comes in Romans 6, which sketches the participationist dimensions of Christ's death. These have been neatly summed up in syllogism form by Daniel Bailey:

> Christ died to sin (Rom. 6:10)

> We died with Christ (6:3–7)

> Therefore: we died to sin (6:2).[22]

---

22. Slightly modified from the account in Moo 1997:354.

To follow the same reverse order of the above: in verse 10, Christ's dying a death to sin refers to the climactic end to the power of sin that the cross brought about; we are then baptized into Christ (Rom. 6:3); therefore, we participate in that decisive end to the power of sin, and so have no possibility of being under its control any longer.

Summary

So to summarize the Pauline data examined here, we can simply repeat the definition offered above: that the gospel is God's account of his saving activity in Jesus the Messiah, in which, by Jesus' death and resurrection, he atones for sin and brings new creation.

Paul and the Synoptics

So in the gospel of Paul we encounter Jesus the Messiah bringing atoning sacrifice and justification, and redemption from the previous evil age into the lordship of Christ. What does this have to do with the preaching of Jesus and the message set out in the fourfold Gospel? A number have, of course, said that the answer is 'very little', and proclaimed Paul a second founder of Christianity.[23] But the differences are only superficial.

Messiahship

First, when it comes to the gospel of the identity of Jesus, there is clearly no disjunction between the epistles and the Gospels. The Fourth Gospel, for example, makes it explicit that the purpose of the document is to convince the reader that the Messiah is Jesus (John 20:30–31). Mark's Gospel has as its heading 'The beginning of the gospel of Jesus Christ' (Mark 1:1). The Gospel of Matthew begins by introducing 'the book of the genealogy of Jesus *Christ*, the *son of David*, the son of Abraham' (Matt. 1:1, my italics). The climactic resurrection appearance in Luke's Gospel has the disappointed disciples lamenting that 'we had hoped that he was the one to redeem Israel'

---

23. E.g. Maccoby 1986.

(Luke 24:21). To this Jesus replies, 'Was it not necessary that the Christ should suffer these things and enter into his glory?' (Luke 24:26; cf. 24:46–47). As in Romans 1, Jesus' Messiahship in the Gospels goes hand in hand with being Son of God, as expressed in particular in the baptism and the transfiguration.[24]

Perhaps even more important for our purposes here, however, is the Gospels' combination of Messiahship with Jesus' identity as the Son of Man. (Interestingly, Paul never uses the title.) In this first section, we can begin by pointing out one aspect which 'Messiah', 'Son of God' and 'Son of Man' (along with 'Lord', the other dominant title) have in common: they all highlight the dominion which Jesus possesses as the divinely installed king. Jesus' Messiahship is highlighted in the references to him as son of David, no mere genealogical titbit, but an accentuation of his role as ruler from the Davidic dynasty. 'Son of God' taps into a similar Davidic connection.[25] Finally, the 'Son of Man' title (as it is, at the very least in the Gospel narratives) evokes the figure in Daniel to whom was given

> dominion
>   and glory and a kingdom,
> that all peoples, nations, and languages
>   should serve him;
> his dominion is an everlasting dominion,
>   which shall not pass away,
> and his kingdom one
>   that shall not be destroyed (Dan. 7:14–15).[26]

---

24. The 'Johannine thunderbolt' (Matt. 11:27/Luke 10:21–22) and the ignorance logion (Mark 13:32; Matt. 24:36) offer further strikingly exalted presentations of the divine sonship of Jesus. The former accentuates the exclusive mutual relationship between Father and Son, even extending to the Son's power in election; the latter places the Son in a heavenly hierarchy between the angels and the Father.

25. See e.g. Marcus 1992:71–72, for discussion of the combination of traditional royal imagery in the sonship language, but with recognition of the divine power implicit in the presentation at the same time.

26. The analysis below has been explained in more detail in Gathercole 2004b.

It is the extraordinary authority that this figure possesses that is revealed by Jesus in the opening of his ministry. To take Mark 2 as an example, Jesus declares the scope of his dominion on two fronts:

the Son of Man has authority on earth to forgive sins . . . (Mark 2:10).

So the Son of Man is lord even of the Sabbath (Mark 2:28).

Both of these far exceed any conventional expectations of a ruler: authority over sin and over divinely sanctified spheres of reality could come only under the aegis of God himself. So the kingly dominion exercised by Jesus the Son of Man here is clearly a point that is emphasized. Jesus' Messiahship is equally central to both Paul and the Gospels.

Jesus' death for the many

The next phase in the ministry of the Son of Man comes in striking contrast to this initial revelation, however. In three of the next references to Jesus' destiny as Son of Man, the authority that has been declared so clearly in the opening events of his ministry is rejected. In a series of passion predictions, Jesus announces that the Son of Man is going to be handed over to the Gentiles and put to death (Mark 8:31; 9:31; 10:45). The first of these is striking in that it is obviously a comment on the nature of Jesus' Messiahship. The last is particularly relevant to our theme because of its overlap with the theme of atonement, which is so prominent in Paul's exposition of the gospel in 1 Corinthians 15. As Mark 10:45 puts it, 'For even the Son of Man came not to be served but to serve, and to give his life as a ransom for many.' This verse is very important in our context for two reasons. To start with, it explains the apparent contradiction between – on the one hand – the enormous scope of Jesus' authority as Son of Man, which we saw was a feature of the opening of his ministry in Mark's Gospel, and – on the other – the fact that this authority has been not only resisted but actually overcome. Why do the people rage against the Lord's anointed one? Well, because apparently they can defeat him. In fact, however, while the Son of Man *revealed* that authority at the outset, it was never his intention to impose that authority finally over that generation; rather, his first coming was to die as the Servant of the Lord.

Why this intention? Because 'the many' need not only the defeat of their enemies but their own lives bought back as well. I have argued elsewhere that one aspect of the background to this 'ransom' language lies in the statements in Exodus 21 and 30, which are concerned with payments for the redemption of life.[27] In addition, there is also more than a passing nod to Isaiah 53, where the Lord lays the iniquity of us all upon the Servant (Isa. 53.6). So Jesus in Mark 10:45 is paying in his death the ransom price for his people who need sins borne by another to avoid death. A similar idea comes in Caiaphas's ironic statement in John's Gospel, where the high priest prophesies that Jesus will die on behalf of and instead of the whole people of God (John 11:20–52).

The statement in Mark 10:45 is not only one among many of Mark's and Jesus' statements about his death, but the one that actually explains the purpose of it. The death of Christ is clearly not incidental to his coming, especially when one considers that in Mark, Jesus' journey to his death occupies almost half the work. The passion in the other Gospels is no less climactic, even if it does not occupy quite the same word count. And this passion is explained, theologically, in this particular statement in Mark 10:45, as the payment of a ransom price (cf. Mark 14:24). As in 1 Corinthians 15, we have the motif of penal substitution, in that Jesus functions both as substitute ('for many') and as the one who pays the price required for sin. In this respect, the ransom motif accentuates the more individual dimension to Markan soteriology; there is perhaps also an implication that those bought by Jesus are those who are predestined to enter the

---

27. See Gathercole 2003:162–164. In Exod. 21, if an Israelite irresponsibly causes death, then he himself should be put to death. However, it is possible, if the family of the deceased consent, that 'he shall *give for the redemption of his life whatever is imposet on him*' (Exod. 21:30; my italics). Similarly, at Moses' census, in order to avoid plague, 'each shall *give a ransom for his life to* the LORD' (Exod. 30:12; my italics).

kingdom.[28] On the other hand, the Son of Man also represents the people of God as a whole. The sequence of Daniel 7 indicates that his relation to the saints of the Most High is analogous in the chapter to the relation between the other kings and their kingdoms. This will be explored further below.

The conquest of the demonic realm and the reign of God

An important parallel to Paul's idea of the destruction of the old world and its new creation comes in the beginning of Jesus' ministry. In Mark 1, Jesus proclaims that the time is fulfilled and the kingdom near, and commands repentance and belief in the gospel. Because Jesus the King has come, the kingdom of God is inaugurated. This means the demolition of the demonic control of the world, and the establishment of God's reign in its place. As a result of the inauguration of God's kingdom, unclean spirits are cast out (Mark 1:21–28), the sick are healed (1:29–34), those with leprosy and the paralysed are cured (1:40–45; 2:1–12). In the course of this, the gospel is preached (1:14–15, 39) and sins are forgiven (2:5, 10). People are commanded to abandon old allegiances, and to follow Jesus. This is how one enters the kingdom.

Scholars have also observed the correspondence between the Son of Man motif and the theme of the kingdom of God. This is understandable given the backdrop in Daniel 7, which joins the two so closely together. The first coming of the Son of Man was a revelation of his authority, but ultimately aimed at Jesus' death; it did nevertheless constitute both the announcement of the defeat of the demonic hold over God's creation and the paradoxical defeat of sin through the death of Jesus. However, the second coming of Jesus will be the occasion of his final vanquishing of sin, when the Son of Man comes in glory, in the power of his angels.

The coming of the kingdom in the gospel thus has the same twofold character as the coming of the Son of Man. The kingdom comes in the person of Jesus in Mark 1. The kingdom is present because the King-Messiah is present. But the rule of Jesus, while

---

28. As suggested already by Schweitzer 1945:352–353; see alternatively Schweitzer 2000:322–323.

exercised for the benefit of many, is not established fully until his second coming. This corresponds to the tension in Paul between God's people experiencing in the present the risen life of Christ, but knowing full liberation and glory only at the end of the age. In the Gospels, too, followers of Jesus are secure in their status of belonging to Christ and already belong to the kingdom, but still await its consummation.

Conclusion

I have suggested here that the similarity between the gospel according to Paul and the gospel according to the evangelists lies not in the equivalence of certain terms, such as 'righteousness of God' in Paul = 'kingdom of God' in the Synoptics. Similarly, I have not taken the approach of harmonizing Paul and the Gospels by, for example, arguing that Paul's use of the language of 'kingdom of God' is much more significant in his thought than is implied by the small number of references. Rather, the unity of their presentations of the gospel can be seen in the broad outlines of these three key themes: (1) the identity of Jesus as Messiah, (2) his work of atoning sacrifice and justification, and (3) his inauguration of a new dominion. These lie at the heart of the apostolic gospel.

© Simon Gathercole, 2006.

6. KERYGMA OR KERYGMATA: IS THERE ONLY ONE GOSPEL IN THE NEW TESTAMENT?

David Peterson

It was James Dunn who first alerted me to the problem of saying that there is 'only one gospel' in the New Testament.[1] As a theological student, I had been much impressed by C. H. Dodd's *The Apostolic Preaching and its Developments*.[2] However, Dunn challenged this approach and presented a more complex analysis of the sources. It would be difficult to estimate the extent to which Dunn's position has impacted New Testament scholarship. Perhaps he was giving expression to patterns of thought that were emerging from different quarters and which continued to have their own impetus and influence. The questions he raises and the solutions he proposes certainly continue to have a contemporary ring. I have heard and read many similar arguments since I first encountered his work. It is for this reason that I want to take issue with his particular presentation, revisiting the 'debate' between Dodd and Dunn (Dodd himself had no opportunity to engage with Dunn's book, having

1. Dunn 1977:11–32.
2. Dodd 1936.

died in September 1973).[3] At the same time, I want to draw together some of the perspectives shared by contributors to the present volume and make some conclusions about gospel presentations in various strands of the New Testament and their interconnection.

Dodd's proposal

C. H. Dodd drew from an analysis of the Pauline letters the following outline of Paul's kerygma (message preached):[4]

- The prophecies are fulfilled and the new age is inaugurated by the coming of Christ.
- He was born of the seed of David.
- He died according to the Scriptures to deliver us out of the present evil age.
- He was buried.
- He rose on the third day according to the Scriptures.
- He is exalted at the right hand of God as Son of God and Lord of living and dead.
- He will come again as Judge and Saviour of all.

---

3. See Dillistone 1977.

4. Dodd took the Greek word 'kerygma' to mean '*what* is preached', whereas Bultmann took it to refer to 'the *act* of preaching' (Bultmann 1952:307). For Bultmann and those who followed him, kerygma was not an enlightening world-view 'flowing out into general truths, nor a merely historical account', but 'by nature, personal address which accosts each individual, throwing the person himself into question by rendering his self-understanding problematic, and demanding a decision of him'. Dunn (1977:12) points out that of the seven occurrences of the word kerygma in the NT some are best understood as denoting the act of preaching (particularly Matt. 12:41/Luke 11:32; 1 Cor. 15:14). However, he rightly argues that statistically *euangelion* (gospel) and *martyria* (witness) are more important than kerygma in the New Testament. In the final analysis we cannot avoid investigating the *content* of the message preached by the earliest Christians, even if it varies to some extent from situation to situation.

Dodd then examined the speeches in Acts attributed to Peter and Paul. The speeches of Peter 'supplement one another, and taken together they afford a comprehensive view of the content of the early kerygma'.[5] In summary, they proclaim:

- The age of fulfilment has dawned.
- This has taken place through the ministry, death and resurrection of Jesus.
- By virtue of his resurrection Jesus has been exalted at the right hand of God, as the messianic head of the new Israel.
- The Holy Spirit in the church is the sign of Christ's present power and glory.
- The messianic age will shortly reach its consummation in the return of Christ.
- Repentance is necessary in order to receive the offer of forgiveness and the Holy Spirit and the promise of 'salvation' (i.e. 'the life of the Age to Come') to those who enter the elect community.

Dodd went on to show the links between the sermon attributed to Paul in Acts 13:16–41 and the Petrine kerygma. He concluded:

> There is nothing specifically Pauline in it, except the term 'justification.' On the other hand, the general scheme, and the emphasis, correspond with what we have found in the epistles, and there is little or nothing in it which could not be documented out of the epistles, except the historical details in the introductory passage (xiii. 16–22) and the specific allusions to the episodes in the Gospel story, and in particular to the ministry of John the Baptist (the fullest account in the New Testament outside the Gospels) and the trial before Pilate.[6]

In short, a comparison of the Pauline letters with the speeches in Acts led Dodd to discover 'a fairly clear and certain outline

---

5. Dodd 1936:21.
6. Dodd 1936:29–30. Dodd offers two reasons why these episodes in the Gospels did not fall wholly outside the range of Paul's interest.

sketch of the preaching of the apostles'.[7] Dodd recognized that, within the New Testament, there is 'an immense range of variety in the interpretation that is given to the kerygma', but he was convinced that 'in all such interpretation, the essential elements of the original kerygma are steadily kept in view'.[8] Despite the diversity he saw, Dodd believed that there was one gospel which could be discerned in the New Testament.

Dunn's response

The kerygma of Jesus

J.D.G. Dunn, however, questioned this approach. The first chapter of his *Unity and Diversity* contains what he calls 'an aerial survey of the most important proclamations of the gospel in the New Testament'.[9] Focusing first on the kerygma of Jesus, he concludes that the characteristic features of Jesus' preaching are threefold:

- He proclaimed the kingdom of God, both its imminence and its presence – Jesus saw himself as the instrument of this end-time rule, but he did not put himself forward as the content of his kerygma.
- He called for repentance and faith in the face of the end-time power and the claim of God – Jesus himself was not the object of faith.
- He offered forgiveness and a share in the messianic feast of the new age with its ethical corollary of love.

This summary of the evidence of the Synoptic Gospels fails to stress the fulfilment motif and makes two questionable claims: Dunn contends that Jesus did not put himself forward as the content of his kerygma and was not himself the object of faith. Dunn's approach needs to be challenged, first because of the evi-

---

7. Dodd 1936:31.
8. Dodd 1936:74.
9. Dunn 1977:13.

dence of the Synoptic Gospels themselves and, second, because his reconstruction of the gospel of Jesus forms the basis for arguing that the apostolic preaching in Acts was profoundly different from Jesus' own preaching.

The fulfilment motif

The fulfilment motif emerges in Jesus' teaching in a number of ways. It is part of the gospel summary in Mark 1:14–15. It appears again in statements about the significance of Jesus' coming (e.g. Matt. 5:17–20; Luke 4:18–21), which are linked to scriptural expectations about the messianic era (e.g. Matt. 5:2–12), and to authoritative teaching, which raises questions about his identity and status in the plan of God (e.g. Matt. 5:21 – 7:29). It occurs in connection with his teaching about John the Baptist and the reaction of his contemporaries, both to John and to himself as John's successor (e.g. Matt. 11:2–30). It surfaces in many of the parables with their biblical and eschatological allusions (e.g. Matt. 13). It is expressed directly in the way Jesus interprets Scripture and applies it to himself and his ministry (e.g. Matt. 21:42–46; 22:41–46; Luke 24:25–27, 44–49).

All this is an important background for reading the speeches in Acts and understanding how the gospel was expounded in the rest of the New Testament. But the fundamental point is that, for Jesus, the fulfilment of God's promises in his own person and work was the first plank of the gospel he proclaimed.

Jesus as the object of faith

While it is true that Jesus in the Synoptic Gospels does not regularly and openly draw attention to himself as the object of faith, he does say things that progressively raise questions about his identity and his role in the saving plan of God. For example, there is a clear challenge to personal discipleship in Mark's Gospel immediately after Jesus' first public proclamation of the gospel. Jesus said to Simon and Andrew, 'Follow me, and I will make you become fishers of men' (Mark 1:16–17). 'To interpret this phrase only as a play on words appropriate to the situation is to fail to appreciate its biblical background and its relevance to the context, which has focused attention on God's eschatological act in sending

Jesus.'[10] God is the fisher of men in passages such as Jeremiah 16:16, Ezekiel 29:4–5, 38:4, Amos 4:2, Habakkuk 1:14–17. Since Jesus has come proclaiming the imminent judgment of God, Simon and Andrew are being summoned to join Jesus in bearing witness to this fact and to call their contemporaries to repentance and faith. But the call is to be a follower first and a collaborator second.

In Mark 2:1–12 (cf. Matt. 9:1–8; Luke 5:17–26), the teachers of the Law are offended by Jesus' claim to be able to forgive sins. Jesus responds by healing the paralytic and indicating that this is a sign that 'the Son of Man has authority on earth to forgive sins'. In effect, he proclaims himself as the one ordained to fulfil the prophecy of Daniel 7:13–14. He is the one destined to provide forgiveness of sins on the day of God's final judgment and is exercising that authority in advance as he forgives sins on earth. This claim is so public and so early in the record of Jesus' ministry that many scholars have doubted its authenticity. Apart from 2:28, which is questioned on similar grounds, the title 'Son of Man' does not enter the Markan account until after the acknowledgment of Jesus as Messiah in 8:29. From that point it appears to provide an important key to Jesus' self-disclosure to his *disciples*. Many scholars therefore propose that we have here an interpolation into a simple healing narrative. Lane calls it 'a parenthetical statement addressed by the evangelist to the *Christian* readers of the Gospel to explain the significance of the closing phase of the healing *for them*.'[11] Hooker similarly argues that 'Mark's account of the story reflects a time when the story was being seen as an example of forgiveness, rather than one particular incident: the authority delegated to Jesus is permanent and of universal scope.'[12]

However, this saying ought to be seen within the general context of Jesus' pattern of self-disclosure, in which there is a tension between action and passivity,[13] involving both secrecy and revelation. Speaking about 'the Son of Man' in the third person,

---

10. Lane 1974:67.

11. Lane 1974:98; cf. Gundry 1993:118–123.

12. Hooker 1991:88. On pp. 88–95 Hooker briefly discusses alternative views.

13. Cf. Stonehouse 1944:50–85; Marshall 1992; Kim 1983.

Jesus is indirectly pointing to himself and hinting at his critical role in the plan of God. The saying is strange enough, and suggestive enough of Old Testament and intertestamental usage of such terminology, to provoke questioning and enquiry. At the same time, it is opaque enough to leave some of his hearers confused and complacent. In this respect it functions like the parables and many of the public sayings of Jesus, drawing out from the crowds those who were challenged to know more about Jesus. There is no reason why Jesus could not have spoken of himself in this way before such an audience, though the meaning and significance of his claim may not have been clear even to his disciples at that point in time. Leaving aside all such critical arguments, we may ask how the earliest Christians came to put such a claim on the lips of Jesus. What part did Jesus himself play in leading his disciples to acknowledge him in this way?

The suffering Son of Man

Mark presents a number of incidents in which Jesus challenges his disciples to consider who he might be, before asking the question at Caesarea Philippi 'Who do people say that I am?' (8:27). Peter's conclusion that he is the Messiah is met with a warning not to tell anyone about him (8:29–30). Jesus then reveals himself as the Son of Man who must suffer many things and be rejected by the elders, the chief priests and the teachers of the Law, and that he must be killed and after three days rise again. The necessity of his suffering as the Son of Man becomes a developing theme in the following chapters (9:12–13, 9:30–32, 10:32–33, 45). Such predictions were so contrary to the kingdom expectations of the disciples that Peter took Jesus aside and began to rebuke him (8:32). Jesus in turn rebuked Peter and said, 'Get behind me, Satan! For you are not setting your mind on the things of God, but on the things of man' (8:33). In other words, Jesus sought to challenge the kingdom expectations of his disciples and bring right into the forefront of their thinking the necessity for his own death and resurrection. Such teaching in Mark's Gospel represents an expansion and development of the summary message revealed in 1:14–15. This fuller gospel presentation shows how the apostolic preaching in Acts came to be so Christ-centred.

The revelation at Caesarea Philippi is then followed by a more personal and comprehensive challenge to discipleship (8:34–38). Attachment to Jesus is shown to have eschatological significance. It is only those who deny themselves and take up their cross to follow Jesus who can lose their life and so be saved. The context makes it clear that salvation has to do with the coming of the Son of Man in the Father's glory with the holy angels (v. 38), which is another way of talking about the kingdom of God coming with power (9:1). Nowhere is the link between a personal faith in Jesus and one's eschatological destiny more clearly expressed than in Mark 8:38: 'Whoever is ashamed of me and of my words in this adulterous and sinful generation, of him will the Son of Man also be ashamed when he comes in the glory of his Father with the holy angels.'

Dunn confuses the picture when he says that Jesus did not put himself forward as the content of his kerygma, nor put himself forward as the object of faith. Although these issues are more explicit in the apostolic preaching exemplified in Acts and the epistles, the Synoptic Gospels show us how Jesus led his disciples from their own kingdom expectations to his own – kingdom expectations in which the suffering Son of Man would be a key to the salvation of all who followed him.

The kerygma in Acts

Dunn concludes that we can recognize within the different sermons reproduced by Acts a regular outline that may be said to provide a solid core which we can call the basic kerygma of the earliest church. The most regular and foundational elements are these:

- Proclamation of the resurrection of Jesus.
- The call for a response to this proclamation for repentance and faith in this Jesus.
- The promise of forgiveness, salvation and Spirit to those who so respond.

This is a more simple outline than the one presented by Dodd, and its very simplicity creates problems, especially when we seek to compare this kerygma with the preaching of Jesus and the kerygma of Paul.

The proclaimer and the proclaimed

Dunn begins his analysis of the material in Acts by saying, 'Jesus proclaimed the kingdom; the sermons in Acts *proclaim Jesus*. Jesus has become the content of the message; the proclaimer has become the proclaimed.'[14] As I suggested previously, this hard and fast distinction between the Gospels and Acts will not do. First, Chris Green has shown us that the kingdom of God remains a key for understanding the gospel in the book of Acts. It is mentioned at significant points in the narrative as a way of describing the preaching of the gospel, concluding with the record of Paul in Rome 'proclaiming the kingdom of God and teaching about the Lord Jesus Christ with all boldness and without hindrance' (28:31).

The kingdom of God was the theological context or framework in which Jesus was proclaimed as Lord and Christ (cf. 20:21–27).[15] Sometimes it is simply stated that the early Christian preachers proclaimed the kingdom (8:12; 19:8; 20:25; cf. 14:22) and some-times it appears that the preaching was exclusively Christological (e.g. 2:14–41; 3:12–26; 4:8–12). Closer examination reveals the extent to which kingdom theology familiar to us from the Gospels has influenced this Christological presentation.

Dodd made an interesting comparison between the summary of Jesus' preaching in Mark 1:14–15 and the Petrine or early Jerusalem kerygma found in Acts:

> The first clause, 'The time is fulfilled,' is expanded in the reference to prophecy and its fulfilment. The second clause, 'The Kingdom of God has drawn near', is expanded in the account of the ministry and death of Jesus, His resurrection and exaltation, all conceived as an eschatological process. The third clause, 'Repent and Believe the Gospel', reappears in

---

14. Dunn 1977:17.

15. Luke brings the two approaches together again in 28:23, where he records that Paul was testifying to the kingdom of God and trying to convince the Jews of Rome about Jesus both from the Law of Moses and the Prophets.

the appeal for repentance and the offer of forgiveness with which the apostolic kerygma closes. Whether we say that the apostolic preaching was modelled on that of Jesus, or that the evangelist formulated his summary of the preaching of Jesus on the model of that of the primitive Church, at any rate the two are identical in purport. The Kingdom of God is conceived as coming in the events of the life, death, and resurrection of Jesus, and to proclaim these facts, in their proper setting, is to preach the Gospel of the Kingdom of God.[16]

This is an important argument, which Dunn does not appear to acknowledge. Furthermore, as I said previously, the difference between the Synoptic Gospels and the preaching in Acts is one of degree. There is a development in the way in which Jesus becomes explicitly the content of the message. At the same time, Luke can still talk about Paul preaching the kingdom of God, 'so that all the residents of Asia heard *the word of the Lord*, both Jews and Greeks' (Acts 19:8–10; my italics). That 'word' has previously been shown to be the message about Jesus as the Messiah who died and rose again in fulfilment of Scripture, to provide the definitive forgiveness of sins and eternal life that are key aspects of the eschatological salvation promised to Israel in the Scriptures (13:16–48).

Dunn thinks it is striking that the actual sermons in Acts contain remarkably few echoes of Jesus' own message and teaching, but then he qualifies that by immediately referring to 8:12; 14:22; 19:8; 20:25, 35; 28:23, 31, where the phrase 'the kingdom of God' is found, or 20:35, where there is an allusion to the otherwise unrecorded saying of Jesus. Dunn says there is hardly any concern shown for the historical Jesus, but then immediately qualifies this by referring to 2:22 and 10:36–39. A difference of emphasis does not establish a discontinuity between Jesus' proclamation of the kingdom and the apostolic proclamation of Jesus and the kingdom in Acts.

Atonement in Acts

A particular point of apparent discontinuity noted by many scholars is the fact that the sermons in Acts concentrate on the

---

16. Dodd 1936:24.

resurrection and there is 'an absence of any theology of the death of Jesus'.[17] Dunn overstates the case here, but then more specifically argues that the historical fact of Jesus' death is not interpreted as a sacrifice for sins in texts such as 2:23, 36; 3:13–15; 4:10; 5:30; 7:52; 10:39; 13:27–28. He contends that the few brief allusions to Jesus as the Servant of the Lord pick up the theme of vindication through suffering, though not vicarious suffering as such (3:13, 26; 4:27, 30; 8:30–35). Dunn also argues that the allusions to Deuteronomy 21:22–23 in Acts 5:30; 10:39 ('hanging him on a tree', cf. 13:29) seem to be intended by Luke to highlight Jesus' shame and disgrace and so serve the same humiliation/vindication motif. Dunn is unwilling to see here any hint of Jesus' bearing the curse of God or shedding his blood for the salvation of his people.

J. B. Green, however, has drawn attention to three texts that are programmatic for explaining how salvation through Christ is made available.[18] The first is in 5:30–32, where Peter proclaims that Jesus' resurrection and exaltation to the right hand of God as 'Prince' (*archēgos*) and 'Saviour' (*sōtēr*) makes it possible for him to offer repentance and forgiveness of sins (cf. 2:38; 3:19–20, 26; 11:18). His death is mentioned in the accusation that the religious authorities 'hanged him on a tree' (5:30; cf. 10:39; 13:29; 1 Pet. 2:24, where similar language is found). In this context, the allusion to Deuteronomy 21:22–23 must mean more than shame and disgrace, suggesting that he was cursed by God. The raising of Jesus proclaims his vindication and ability to save from God's judgment even those who condemned him to death. While there may not be an articulated theology of Christ becoming a curse for us here (cf. Gal. 3:13–14), such an atoning dimension to his death could easily be argued or assumed from the cumulative effect of the argument in 5:30–31. 'These allusions serve to locate Jesus' death firmly in the necessity of God's purpose. The ultimate disgrace, the curse from God, is antecedent to exaltation.'[19]

---

17. Dunn 1977:17; cf. Conzelmann 1960:200–201; Tyson 1986; Sylva 1990.
18. Green 1998.
19. Green 1998:101.

Green's second text is Acts 10:43, where the witness is less direct, but quite similar. Jesus' ability to forgive sins is said to be in accordance with the testimony of 'all the prophets'. Green argues that the solution to this puzzling allusion to the prophets is 'Luke's consistent view that at his exaltation Jesus received the title "Lord" and with it the divine prerogative to offer salvation'.[20] That is more obviously so in 2:33, which is the third text to which Green draws attention. In its context, this affirms that the prophecy from Joel cited in 2:21 is fulfilled in and by the exalted Lord Jesus Christ. But what other scriptures could be included in the testimony of 'all the prophets?'

Isaiah 53 appears to be a key text influencing the soteriology of Luke-Acts, though the quotations in Luke 22:37 and Acts 8:32–23 do not make explicit reference to vicarious atonement. They draw attention to *significant aspects* of Jesus' suffering (the innocent one suffering the death of a transgressor, led like a sheep to the slaughter), suggesting that these events should be understood in terms of Isaiah's redemptive theology. The theme of Jesus' vindication in the apostolic preaching belongs within this framework.[21]

The farewell scene in the upper room (Luke 22:14–38) provides a theological basis for interpreting the events to follow and a justification for the claim that forgiveness of sins can be proclaimed in the name of the exalted Christ (24:44–47). In the flow of the narrative, this points the readers of Luke's second volume towards a redemptive view of Jesus' death, even if this is not always articulated in the recorded sermons. In Paul's farewell address to the Ephesian elders, as in Jesus' discourse in the upper room, the shedding of the Messiah's blood is the means by which the New Covenant is inaugurated and Messiah's people are

---

20. J. B. Green, 'The Death of Jesus, God's Servant', in Sylva 1990:1–28 (9). Green expounds this 'exaltation-soteriology' on pp. 9–11 and then seeks to relate this to a number of other NT texts where the salvific character of Jesus' resurrection in tandem with the cross is highlighted (pp. 11–12). He then shows parallels with the literature of late Judaism, where exalted human beings carry out soteriological functions (pp. 12–18).

21. See Peterson 2004:60–71.

sanctified for their share with him in his eternal inheritance (20:28). This is the heart of 'the gospel of the grace of God', which Paul preached in their midst (20:24; cf. 14:3, 'the word of his grace'), and which Peter defended at the Jerusalem Council (15:11, 'saved through the grace of the Lord Jesus'). It is the same 'message of his grace' (20:32) that is able to sustain the church in the face of persecution and false teaching. In other words, atonement theology in Luke 22 and Acts 20 is the basis for proclaiming forgiveness and the saving grace of God. It is the means by which the eschatological people of God is formed and sustained.

In terms of narrative development, particularly the placement of key speeches, references to salvation by the grace of God, allusions to Jesus as the Servant of the Lord, and the portrayal of his suffering and vindication in terms reminiscent of Isaiah 53, Luke presents Jesus' death as an atonement for sin. Only on this basis can the risen Lord provide the definitive forgiveness of sins that inaugurates the New Covenant and secures for believers the promised eternal inheritance (20:32; 26:18). Although the resurrection is prominent in Luke's presentation of the early preaching, and the atoning significance of Jesus' death is not always stressed, the various ways in which the saving benefits of Jesus' death and resurrection are presented (e.g. 3:17–26; 10:42–43; 13:38–41) give a comprehensive and cumulative picture of early Christian thinking about the saving significance of those great events.

Eschatology in Acts

Dunn also argues that the sermons in Acts lack the tension between fulfilment and imminent consolation that was such a prominent feature of Jesus' proclamation of the kingdom, and which is equally strong in Paul's message: 'The sense of its imminence barely squeezes through Luke's formulation in Acts 3:20f., and the day of judgement hardly seems to offer more than a distant threat – certainly not an immediate crisis such as Jesus envisaged (10:42, 17:31, 24:25).'[22] Dunn argues that, apart from 2:15–21 and 3:24, the notion of a realized eschatology is wholly

---

22. Dunn 1977:18.

absent from the book of Acts. He concludes that Luke has suppressed or ignored this element of the early kerygma, 'presumably because the lapse of time and delay of the parousia made it less appropriate'.[23]

Dunn offers an immediate qualification to this argument by noting that the sharing of goods in Acts 2 and 4 is best explained as an expression of eschatological enthusiasm: property was sold 'without much thought for the needs of a year hence, for the Christ would have returned before then'.[24] As with the theology of atonement, we need to go beyond the precise formulations in the sermons and consider the pattern of belief reflected in Luke's narrative as a whole. Luke presumably expected the sermonic material to be interpreted within that framework. John Nolland has argued convincingly that

> Luke continued to expect the parousia within his own generation. He sees the kingdom of God as having both a present (and developing) as well as a climactic future dimension. He does not think in terms of sharply delineated periods in salvation-history: the same story keeps repeating, but in different keys and with a definite sense of escalation towards a climax represented by the parousia.[25]

The ascended Christ

Dunn goes on to argue that there is hardly any role attributed to the exalted Jesus in Acts. He bestows the Spirit of Pentecost (Acts 2:33) and will return as judge at the end (10:42; 17:31). Jesus is the authority behind those who act in the name of Jesus (e.g. 2:38; 3:6; 4:10, 30; 8:16) and he appears in a number of visions in which guidance is given to the earliest believers (7:55–56; 9:10; 18:9; 22:17–18; 23:11; 26:16, 19). Nevertheless, for Dunn, there is nothing of the 'rich sense of union between the believer and the exalted Lord which is such a feature of the messages of Paul and John'.[26] This is

---

23. Dunn 1977:19.
24. Dunn 1977:19.
25. Nolland 1998:81.
26. Dunn 1977:19.

a weak argument, which has been opposed by a number of scholars. For example, R. F. O'Toole concludes his research with this summary:

> The risen Lord acts and is present to the whole life of his church. He leads the Christians. Their mission is Christ's mission. He gives his followers their mission and directs them. When they are persecuted, he encourages, supports, and protects them. His power enables them to perform miracles. When they preach, he preaches; when they are heard, he is heard. Their salvation, a present experience and reality, comes only from him. They are baptized in his name and realize his presence in the Eucharist. Certainly, the Father and the Spirit are active, but a church without considerable activity on the part of the risen Christ is not Lukan.[27]

Even the verses quoted by Dunn indicate a sense of the presence of the exalted Christ and his direction of events in the early church.[28] If there is more of the 'rich sense of union between the believer and the exalted Lord' in the writings of Paul and John, that has very much to do with the context in which they were writing. However, no-one would deny that experiences of the Holy Spirit are a key aspect of the theology of Acts, and Luke makes it very clear that it is the Spirit poured out *by Jesus*, in effect Jesus' way of continuing to be present with and to guide and bless his church.

Dunn sees an extensive overlap with other parts of the New Testament with respect to the promises of the gospel: forgiveness, salvation and the gift of the Holy Spirit are often mentioned in Acts and are paralleled in other strains of the New Testament. The call for repentance and faith in the kerygma of Acts is familiar, though

---

27. O'Toole 1981:498; cf. O'Toole 1979; Parsons 1987.
28. Dunn's *Baptism in the Holy Spirit* (Dunn 1970b:38–102) is particularly strong on the regenerative work of the Spirit in Acts, and the experiential dimension of the gift of the Spirit. In this respect, his earlier work seems to argue for closer links with Paul's writings and the Fourth Gospel on this subject.

interestingly the demand for repentance more closely parallels the teaching of Jesus than John and Paul. Luke's emphasis on faith is closely paralleled by both the Fourth Gospel and the Pauline letters.

Contextual preaching

To conclude my remarks on Acts, I want to make some observations about the structure and contents of key sermons and to compare them with Dodd's summary outline of the apostolic kerygma. I have taken his outline of the Petrine speeches and applied this also to the sermon preached by Paul in the synagogue at Pisidian Antioch. Context undoubtedly influences the shape and focus of these speeches, but it is remarkable that certain themes regularly emerge in them all. Paul's Athenian address (17:22–31) is a special case, which is generally not included here, though certain points of overlap are noted.[29]

The age of fulfilment theme appears first in Acts 2:15–21, where Peter uses Joel 2:28–32 to explain the Pentecost event. However, the note of fulfilment is sounded again when the 'definite plan and foreknowledge of God' is mentioned in connection with Jesus' betrayal and death (2:23), and the meaning of his resurrection and ascension is explored in terms of other scriptural texts (2:24–36). Peter's second sermon is driven by the need to explain the healing of the man who was lame and to highlight the authority of the 'name' of Jesus in the process (3:16).[30] However, even this occa-

---

29. The theme of fulfilment, which would have been inappropriate for such an audience, is replaced in Acts 17 by a biblical perspective on creation, God's character and his purpose for humanity in the created order. Luke's brief record of this address nevertheless concludes with the proclamation of Jesus' resurrection, the coming judgment and the need for repentance. Key elements in Paul's gospel are preceded by a biblical apologetic, based more on the early chapters of Genesis than prophetic expectations.

30. This 'name of Jesus' theology emerges again in a further defence of the healing of the lame man (4:8–12), where the fulfilment aspect of the kerygma is expressed in terms of Ps. 118:22 and the death and resurrection of Jesus is said to achieve a salvation that is unexplained in the context, but which has been expounded in the two preceding sermons.

sional setting moves Peter to begin with a reference to 'the God of Abraham, the God of Isaac, and the God of Jacob, the God of our fathers' (3:13) and to conclude with a reference to the fulfilment of the promise to Abraham in the sending of Jesus to Israel (3:25–26). Other important scriptural allusions in this sermon occur in relation to the glorification of Jesus as the rejected Servant of the Lord (3:13–15, 18; cf. Isa. 52:13 – 53:12) and the promised restoration of all things (3:20–21; cf. Isa. 65:17–25). The fulfilment theme only appears briefly at the climax of the message preached to Cornelius and his household (10:42–43), and only by allusion to scriptural themes in the brief response to the Sanhedrin in 5:30–32. Yet it constitutes the basis of the first main portion of Paul's sermon in the synagogue at Pisidian Antioch (13:16–25) and reappears as an essential part of his Christological exposition (13:32–37) and warning to the hearers (13:40–41).

The ministry, death, and resurrection of Jesus is fundamental to every gospel proclamation, but with different degrees of emphasis. The fullest accounts are found in 2:22–24, 10:36–42, 13:26–31 (even preceded by details about the significance of the ministry of John the Baptist in 13:24–25). The focus in 3:13–15, 4:10–12, 5:30–31 is rather more on the betrayal, death and glorification of Jesus as the Lord's servant. This focus is specifically linked to an appeal for repentance on the part of those who crucified Jesus and is accompanied by the offer of forgiveness and salvation (though this offer is not confined to such contexts). Exclusive reference to the resurrection of Jesus and its implications is found only in 17:30–31. It is important to notice how the cross and resurrection are normally closely linked in the apostolic preaching.

The exaltation of Jesus at the right hand of God, as the Messianic head of the new Israel is explicitly mentioned in 2:33–36, where it is closely linked with the theme of *the Holy Spirit in the church as the sign of Christ's present power and glory*. In this programmatic sermon, Jesus is proclaimed as 'both Lord and Christ', with the first title indicating his identity in relation to the prophecy of Joel 2:32 and the second in relation to the prediction of Psalm 110:1. Peter's second sermon is much more focused on explaining a healing in the name of Jesus and offering forgiveness and a share in the messianic restoration of all things to those who 'killed the Author of life'. His exaltation is more specifically as the rejected Servant of the Lord in 3:13–15 and the Holy Spirit is possibly alluded to in the promise of 'times of refreshing' before the return of the Messiah and the ultimate restoration (3:20–21). The heavenly exaltation is not explicitly mentioned in 4:10–12, though it could be implied from the use of Psalm 118:22. Exaltation to the right hand of God to be 'Leader and Saviour' is stressed in 5:31, and the promise of the Holy Spirit is closely linked with this proclamation in 5:32. The exaltation of Jesus may be implied from the description of him as 'Lord of all' in 10:36 and the declaration that he is 'the one appointed by God to be judge of the living and the dead'. The Holy Spirit is not offered to the household of Cornelius, though the text implies that the preacher was interrupted by the actual coming of the Spirit on those who heard (10:44–46; cf. 10:38, Jesus himself was anointed with the Holy Spirit for his earthly ministry). The messianic kingship of Jesus is emphasized in 13:23, 32–37, though the ascension as a sequel to the resurrection is not mentioned. Here again the Holy Spirit is not mentioned and, as in 3:17–21, 4:11–12, 10:43, the focus is on the offer of forgiveness or participation in eschatological salvation through Jesus.

The idea that *the messianic age will shortly reach its consummation in the return of Christ* is most fully explained in 3:20–21, where it is part of a sequence explaining how the present experience of healing and forgiveness is an anticipation of the promised restoration of all things. Peter introduces the theme of Jesus as 'the one appointed by God to be judge of the living and the dead' (10:42), without linking this to any promise of his return. In the narrative of Acts, Stephen's vision of Jesus as the Son of Man (7:56) and Paul's proclamation of Jesus as the judge (17:31) help to confirm the view that the salvation so often mentioned means rescue from the coming judgment of God (cf. 2:20–21, where this theological context is established; and 3:23, where it is indicated in a different way). The offer of forgiveness is similarly to be understood within that eschatological or kingdom-of-God framework.

Repentance is necessary in order to receive the offer of forgiveness and the Holy Spirit and the promise of 'salvation' (i.e. 'the life of the age to come') to those who enter the elect community. In one way or another, this is made clear in all the recorded sermons (2:37–39; 3:17–21; 4:12; 5:31; 10:43; 13:38–39). The offer of salvation varies with the context, as does the presentation of the person and work of Christ. But the reader of Acts is surely meant to discern the interconnections and gain a cumulative picture of what the apostolic gospel proclaimed and promised.

So I would simplify Dodd's outline by combining some of his points and applying his outline to the Petrine and Pauline speeches addressing those with knowledge of the scriptural basis for the gospel message. The evidence shows the wisdom of Dodd's conclusion that these speeches 'supplement one another, and taken together they afford a comprehensive view of the content of the early kerygma'.[31] Dodd's summary is weak with respect to the theological significance attached to Jesus' death and resurrection in the apostolic sermons. Paul's preaching to pagan audiences has a different starting point (e.g. 14:15–17; 17:22–29), though his preaching of Jesus and the resurrection ultimately leads him to proclaim the need for repentance in the light of God's impending judgment by Christ (17:18, 30–31; cf. 1 Thess. 1:9–10).

The kerygma of Paul

Dunn concludes his brief introductory treatment of the Pauline letters with the claim that 'Paul had a very clear idea of what the gospel of Christ was. But his understanding and expression of it did not take any final or fixed form.'[32] He bases this claim first on the argument that Paul recognized the validity of other proclamations and called them also 'gospel'. In particular, he refers to Paul's distinction between his 'gospel to the uncircumcised' and Peter's 'gospel to the circumcised' (Gal. 2:7).

However, it is surely missing Paul's point in this passage to say that there were two separate messages. The Jerusalem apostles 'added nothing' to Paul's gospel on this occasion (2:6) and perceived God's calling for Paul to take the *same* gospel to the Gentiles that they had been entrusted with to take to the Jews (2:7–9). When

31. Dodd 1936:21.
32. Dunn 1977:26.

Paul later rebuked Peter for his behaviour in Antioch (Gal. 2:11–14), it was not because he was bringing another gospel into the situation. Peter and those who followed his example were acting hypocritically and 'not in step with the truth of the gospel' (2:14, *ouk orthopodousin pros tēn alētheian tou euangeliou*). It is true that Paul calls the message of his opponents in the Galatian churches 'a different gospel' (1:6, *heteron euangelion*), but he immediately qualifies this by saying that they were actually trying to 'distort the gospel of Christ' (1:7, *metastrepsai to euangelion*). Paul insists that there is only one true gospel of Christ (sometimes called 'the gospel of God'), which neither he nor an angel from heaven is at liberty to change (1:8–9)! Dunn finally acknowledges this, observing that in several situations Paul 'resolutely opposed forms of gospel which other believers regarded as authentic and called them "no gospel"'.[33]

Dunn goes on to say that Paul's kerygma took diverse forms as circumstances determined, using 1 Corinthians 9:19–23 as a supportive text. But surely Paul's modification of his behaviour in various situations was to enable people from different contexts to trust in the same gospel. Dunn also argues that Paul's gospel 'developed over the years altering in emphasis and tone'.[34] One particular example of this is the supposed development in Paul's eschatological orientation, from the imminent parousia emphasis of the earlier letters to the calm acceptance of the possibility that he might die before Jesus returns (Phil. 1:20ff.). It is notoriously difficult to set the perceived differences in Paul's teaching in a chronological sequence. Contextual reasons for differences of emphasis and tone appear to have existed from the beginning of his ministry (e.g. compare his exposition of the gospel in Galatians with what he writes at approx-

---

33. Dunn 1977:26. However, this leads Dunn to surmise that Paul would have been unhappy with the Jewish Christian kerygma of Matthew and James. He concludes from this that there are kerygmata in the NT that appear to be incompatible. On p. 24 he rightly draws attention to Paul's attack on the 'different gospel' of his opponents in 2 Cor. 10 – 13, but it is unsatisfactory on the basis of so little argument to claim that Paul would have been unhappy with Matthew and James.

34. Dunn 1977:26.

imately the same time in 1–2 Thessalonians). How can we know that Paul accepted the possibility of his death only preceding the parousia when he was finally in a Roman prison? And does this really amount to a significant loss of imminent end-expectancy?[35]

Turning to the actual structure and content of the Pauline kerygma, Dunn argues that 'Jesus as risen was probably the most prominent feature of Paul's gospel (Rom. 1:3f.; 4:24f.; 8:34; 10:9; 1 Cor. 15:3–11; 1 Thess. 1:10; cf. 2 Tim. 2:8).'[36] The death of Christ receives far more prominence than in Acts (Rom. 3:24–25; 4:25; 1 Cor. 1:23; 2:2; 15:3; 2 Cor. 5:14–21; Gal. 3:1), and 1 Thessalonians 1:10 and 2 Thessalonians 2:5 are 'sufficient proof that the imminent parousia was an integral part of Paul's missionary proclamation, during the first half of his missionary career at any rate'.[37]

The most distinctive and characteristic expressions of Paul's gospel are his emphasis on Jesus as Lord and on the exalted Christ as representative of a new humanity ('the last Adam' – see particularly 1 Cor. 15:20–23, 45–49),

> so that conversion means entering into union with Christ (e.g. Rom. 6:3; 1 Cor. 12:13; Gal. 2:19–20; Col. 3:1, 3), and so that believers are his body (Rom. 12:5; 1 Cor. 12:27) and live, worship, conduct themselves 'in Christ', 'in the Lord' (phrases which occur more than 160 times in Paul's writings).[38]

Dunn contends that the essence of Christianity for Paul is acceptance by God (justification) in an intimate relationship,

---

35. Cf. Lowe 1941:129–142; Bruce 1981:300–313; Perriman 1989:512–521; Witherington 1997:171–186.

36. Dunn 1977:22. It is unfortunate that Dunn does not draw attention to the other points made in some of the passages he cites. So e.g. Rom. 1:2 highlights the theme of scriptural fulfilment as the basis for the Christological message, Rom. 4:25 couples 'delivered up for our trespasses' with 'raised for our justification' and 1 Cor. 15:3–11 brings in the note of scriptural fulfilment and the death of Christ 'for our sins', together with the proclamation of the resurrection.

37. Dunn 1977:22.

38. Dunn 1977:22.

entered into and lived in by faith on man's side, made possible and
empowered by the gift of grace, the gift of the Spirit (see particularly Rom.
3:21 – 5:21; Gal. 2:16 – 4:7). This seems to be the core of Paul's kerygma,
distinctive both in its central emphases and in its developed expression.[39]

The last sentence provides a helpful starting point for evaluat-
ing Dunn's position. There are contexts in which various
kerygmatic and confessional formulae seem to identify the core of
Paul's kerygma (e.g. Rom. 1:2–4; 1 Cor. 15:1–11; Gal. 1:1–5).
However, as Simon Gathercole has argued, Paul is at pains in a
passage like 1 Corinthians 15:1–11 to show the harmony of his
gospel with that of the other apostolic witnesses. Far from being
distinctive and different from the testimony of the Gospel writers,
Paul's gospel is 'God's account of his saving activity in Jesus the
Messiah, in which, by Jesus' death and resurrection he atones for
sin and brings new creation'. It is 'God's account' because it is 'in
accordance with the Scriptures', or explained and applied in the
light of Scripture (cf. Rom. 1:2; 16:25–26). It is kingdom of God
theology because it proclaims both the present rule of Jesus as
Messiah and the hope of his coming again in power and glory.

As well as sharing the core elements of the gospel with other
New Testament witnesses, Paul was also the great theologian of
the gospel, who explored and developed the implications of the
core message in a whole range of practical situations, in each of
his letters. It is not correct to identify each of the trajectories that
Paul pursues as gospel in its own right. There may have been
different ways in which Paul proclaimed the gospel, putting the
emphasis on different elements in various contexts, but there is a
controlling core by which Paul assessed whether a teaching was
consistent with the gospel or not.

Gathercole's analysis of that core is simpler than Dodd's,
though they overlap in certain respects. I have also attempted to
summarize and compare Dunn's rather diffuse comments on
Paul's basic kerygma. Dunn's outline as I have displayed it is closer
to Gathercole than to Dodd:

---

39. Dunn 1977:22–23.

Gathercole	Dodd	Dunn
Who Jesus is		
Royal Messiah and Son of God.	The prophecies are fulfilled and the new age is inaugurated by the coming of Christ, who was born of the seed of David.	Jesus is the Messiah, the Son of God and Lord.[40]
What Jesus accomplished		
Atonement and justification in the cross and resurrection.	He died according to the Scriptures to deliver us out of the present evil age, he was buried and rose on the third day according to the Scriptures.	Jesus crucified and risen, as representative of a new humanity, provides acceptance by God in an intimate relationship.
What Jesus inaugurated		
A new creation involving rescue from the power of sin.	He is exalted at the right hand of God as Son of God and Lord of the quick and the dead. He will come again as Judge and Saviour of men.	Jesus will return to consummate God's kingdom purposes.[41]

40. Dunn 1977:57, 205–216, insists that it is the *historical person* of Jesus who is confessed in terms of his *present status*. On p. 58 he argues that these three titles were used in different circumstances, the first in Jewish Palestine, the second in a Hellenistic–Jewish situation, and the third among Gentiles. However, this is a debatable distinction.

41. Dunn 1977:22, 325–328, 345–346, sees this as an integral part of Paul's missionary proclamation only during the first part of his missionary career.

Dodd's approach reflects more precisely the wording of gospel summaries such as Romans 1:2–4, 1 Corinthians 15:3–4, with elements from other passages attached (e.g. Rom. 2:16; 8:31–34; 10:8–9; Gal. 1:4; 3:1; 4:1–6). It also highlights in a more creedal fashion the great gospel events by which the identity of Jesus and his role in the divine plan is revealed. Dodd's first point about the prophecies being fulfilled and the new age being inaugurated by the coming of Christ provides a more obvious link with the gospel presentations in Acts. Gathercole's approach is more explicitly soteriological. The Pauline expression 'according to the Scriptures', which is quoted by Dodd, implies an interpretative framework for the events proclaimed, though Dodd does not explore this. I suggest the following summary of the Pauline position:

> Paul's gospel essentially proclaims the eschatological and saving significance of the person and work of Jesus Christ, in the light of scriptural expectations, and offers people a share in the benefits through repentance and faith in the glorified Lord Jesus.

The kerygma of John

Dunn first notes the emphasis on faith in the Fourth Gospel, citing 20:31 as a key to the evangelist's purpose: 'so that you may believe that Jesus is the Christ, the Son of God, and that by believing you may have life in his name'. John never speaks of repentance, though it appears obvious in certain contexts that belief involves repentance; namely, a reorientation of life in relation to Jesus as the Christ and the Son of God. However, it is with respect to Christology that we may see the greatest differences between John's Gospel and the Synoptic presentation of Jesus. Even in John 1, we are confronted with the titles *Lamb of God, Messiah, Son of God, King of Israel, Son of Man*; whereas, in the Synoptic Gospels, Jesus' identity is only gradually revealed as time goes on. In John's Gospel there are the famous I AM claims of Jesus (6:35; 8:12; 10:7; 10:11; 11:25; 14:6; 15:1) and other expressions of the self-consciousness of Jesus, particularly about his pre-existence (e.g. 3:13; 6:38; 8:38, 58; 10:36; 17:5, 24).

Much has been written about the differences between the Synoptics and the Fourth Gospel.[42] Dunn believes that John was seeking to give a true picture of the historical Jesus as he now perceived him – 'the historical Jesus as John now sees him to be, the historical Jesus with the glory that was to be his by virtue of his death, resurrection and ascension, already visible in his earthly life (see particularly 1:14, 2:11, 11:4, 12:23, 13:31, 17:5)'.[43] Dunn is right to observe the way in which the various strands of the New Testament relate the historical Jesus and the exalted Christ. The Synoptics, though presenting Jesus in the light of his resurrection and subsequent glory, do not let the two pictures merge to the same extent that John does.

Another important characteristic theme in John is the 'life' terminology – verb and noun occur sixty-seven times in the Johannine literature. These words occur regularly in the Pauline letters and less frequently in Acts. John makes little or no use of the concepts of forgiveness, justification and salvation, but he does link the promise of life closely with the Spirit and his talk of mutual abiding has close parallels to Paul's idea of union with Christ. It is when Dunn begins to talk of these interconnections that he rightly concludes:

> Perhaps then we ought simply to recognize all these as broadly
> equivalent expressions of kerygmatic promise. Their diversity as between
> Acts, Paul and John was presumably determined more by the personal
> preferences of the proclaimer and the appropriateness of the language
> to the situation addressed than by differences of substance and content
> in the promise itself.[44]

Where the Johannine kerygma becomes distinctive is in the way it presents the promise of life as a sharp either/or: 'The hearer must choose life or death and, if he chooses life, he passes at that moment from death to life, leaving death and judgement behind

---

42. Most helpfully, see Blomberg 2001a, 2001b.

43. Dunn 1997:27.

44. Dunn 1977:28.

(3:36, 5:24, 11:25–26, 1 John 3:14, 5:12).'[45] Dunn observes that
such clear-cut antitheses are typical of John's message. The contrast between light and darkness, sight and blindness, truth and
falsehood, spirit and flesh abound within John's literature.
Following on from Paul Woodbridge's examination of the link
between the kingdom of God and eternal life, I would argue that
we can see here a blending of the kingdom of God perspectives of
the Synoptics with the Johannine life terminology. Furthermore,
we can see a fulfilment motif in the Fourth Gospel paralleling the
Synoptics, but with the added feature of images applied to Jesus
from the Old Testament such as temple, bread, light, shepherd,
vine and resurrection, showing how he is the fulfilment of God's
saving plan for Israel and the nations.

Conclusions

Dunn argues that there is a common element present in these
different proclamations: 'They give expression in their different
ways to something we can call a common kerygma.'[46] There are
three components to this core kerygma: first, there is the proclamation of the risen, exalted Christ; second, there is the call for faith, for
acceptance of the proclamation and commitment to the Jesus proclaimed; and, third, there is the promise held out to faith whether it
be in terms of forgiveness, salvation, life or the Holy Spirit.

So, Dunn highlights the unity of the post-Easter kerygmata,
while recognizing the considerable diversity of exposition or
explanation within the various strands of the New Testament.
However, he excludes any reference to the death of Jesus and its
significance and in this summary plays down the eschatological
dimension. He also makes 'the call for faith' the second part
of the core kerygma, which he has not argued previously.[47]

---

45. Dunn 1977:28.

46. Dunn 1977:29–30.

47. Jesus taught that 'repentance and forgiveness of sins' would be preached
    in his name to all nations (Luke 24:47) and Peter proclaimed that God had

Furthermore, Dunn says that this 'gospel' must be understood as
an abstraction. 'No New Testament writer proclaims this kerygma
as such. No New Testament writer reduces the kerygma to this
core. The basic kerygma in each of the cases examined above is
larger than this core. They share these common elements but in
different proportions.'[48]

A gospel summary is only an abstraction if it expresses the bare
minimum of commonality between the various kerygmata in the
New Testament. However, it is no abstraction to say that there was
a 'simple' gospel proclaimed by Jesus (Mark 1:14–15; cf. Matt.
4:17), which he explained and expanded throughout his ministry in
parables and other forms of teaching. This was particularly developed for his disciples in the period after their confession of his
Messiahship, focusing on the necessity of his death and resurrection (e.g. Mark 8:27 – 9:1). Jesus' gospel was given full and final
expression after those great events had taken place, including its
scriptural foundation and its implications for the nations (cf. Luke
24:25–27, 44–49; Acts 1:1–8). This gospel was developed and proclaimed by the apostolic writers and preachers in a variety of
contexts, with different emphases and different applications.

Dunn's approach is too minimalist with regard to the common
elements and the degree to which various expressions or proclamations of the gospel in Acts are actually saying the same thing in
a different way. In this respect, Dodd's work is more helpful. Dunn
further concludes that no New Testament evangelist actually
preached this simple core kerygma that he has extracted from the
material. However, there are minimal gospel summaries in Acts,
which may have been preached exactly as recorded because of
the constraints of the situation (e.g. 4:10–12; 5:30–32). The core
kerygma appears more fully in other contexts, but the briefer

---

exalted Jesus to his right hand 'to give repentance to Israel and forgiveness
of sins' (Acts 5:31). It could be argued that faith and repentance are made
possible by the work of Christ and are therefore offered to people in the
gospel as a gracious possibility: they are not simply the required response
to the gospel.

48. Dunn 1977:30.

summaries are clear and faithful representations of these more comprehensive presentations.

Turning back to the Synoptic Gospels, Dunn argues that it is much more difficult to speak of a unity between the post-Easter kerygma and the kerygma of Jesus. Here again, I would want to argue that the book of Acts represents a transitional phase in which the connections between the post-Easter kerygma and the kerygma of Jesus can be traced. There is a tendency in Acts scholarship to be sceptical about the historicity of Luke's narrative and the sermons that he records. Liberal scholarship sees the heavy hand of Luke imposing his view of things on all the material. However, I would contend that we have here a genuine collection of testimonies from the early church, which Luke has edited and presented within the framework of his own theological interests and perspectives. The book of Acts is a key for answering Dunn's question about the continuity between Jesus the proclaimer and Jesus the proclaimed.

Dunn is absolutely right to assert that we cannot go back behind the post-Easter proclamation to sum up Christianity in terms of the Sermon on the Mount or the parable of the prodigal son. Nor can we loosen the teaching of Jesus from the teaching of Paul, as some would have us do, hoping for a simple and unadorned gospel of the kingdom of God with its supposed social and political priorities. Dunn is right again to conclude that 'the kerygmata of Acts and Paul, and the different way of John, demonstrate that the first Christians were not concerned simply to reproduce the message of Jesus'.[49]

I am therefore grateful that Dunn has concluded that 'there is a unifying strand which holds all the NT kerygmata together and enables us to grasp the distinctive character of the earliest Christian gospel'.[50] He is absolutely right to affirm that, in the concrete situation, the actual gospel was much more closely defined and larger in content than the abstract and artificial core he has identified. I would argue that the summary I gave of the kerygma of Paul works

49. Dunn 1977:31.
50. Dunn 1977:32.

also for the evidence of Acts: the apostolic gospel proclaims the eschatological and saving significance of the person and work of Jesus Christ, in the light of scriptural expectations, and offers people a share in the benefits through repentance and faith in the glorified Lord Jesus. In different ways, the Synoptic and Johannine Gospels present the same basic message, expressed in an essentially narrative form, the Synoptic framework more closely representing the way the message was unfolded in the ministry of Jesus.

Dunn insists that

> any attempt to find a single, once for all, unifying kerygma is bound to fail, for the concrete situation *always* calls forth a more closely defined and larger kerygma – a form of proclamation which, in the concrete situation, cannot be boiled down to the unifying core without losing its meaning and its relevance to the concrete situation.[51]

There may indeed be legitimate differences of expression and application, but this does not mean that we are free to invent our own version of the gospel. Nor does it mean that we can simply opt for one New Testament expression of the gospel over against any other. The diversity of gospel presentation and application in the New Testament establishes parameters for us beyond which we cannot go if we wish to be apostolic and orthodox Christians. That same diversity challenges us to work at the interface of the different gospel presentations, to understand how they cohere and how our presentation of the gospel to different situations can be enriched.

This raises a number of practical questions that readers might like to consider. For example, in what contexts is it most appropriate to preach the gospel in terms of eternal life rather than in terms of the kingdom of God? What is gained and what is lost by simply focusing on one perspective at the expense of the other? Why does Peter present the gospel in one way in Acts 2 and in another way to what must have been a fairly similar audience in Acts 3? What can we learn about apologetics and evangelism from the example of Paul in Acts 17:22–31? What is gained and what is

---

51. Dunn 1977:32.

lost by teaching a core kerygma to a group of Christians and encouraging them to go out and present it in a variety of contexts? Is it always necessary to have some explanation of the atonement for there to be a genuine gospel presentation? Is preaching the resurrection the same as preaching the exaltation of Christ and its implications? To what extent should an evangelistic message expound the scriptural basis of the gospel and provide people with an eschatological framework?

7. WORSHIP, OUR MISSION: RESPONDING TO THE GOD WHO HAS RESCUED US – A SERMON ON DEUTERONOMY 6:4–5[1]

James Robson

Introduction

A friend of mine emailed me some months back and asked me to come and speak at his church. I replied 'Yes,' and put it in my diary. It was only three weeks or so ago, though, that he told me the title: 'Worship – our Mission'. It was the first in a series of three, and he said he was leaving it to me to choose a Bible passage.

This left me a bit anxious. For one thing, a topic without a passage means that there is the risk of squeezing a passage to fit the topic or to give the requisite answer. For another, the title can mean different things to different people. After all, 'worship' is used for worshipping God in song; but also, of course, all of our life is

---

1. Preached at Oak Hill Chapel, on 22 September 2005. Since this a sermon, not an academic paper, I have tried to keep the 'feel' of a sermon, and have not included footnotes – apart from this one! Nonetheless, my indebtedness to a number of articles (Moberly 1990, 1999; Wright 1991; Block 2004), as well as the standard commentaries should be evident.

worship. Similarly, 'mission' is a fluid word. It can speak of what the church should be up to in the world, or it could be something more individual, such as 'our calling in life'. My friend helpfully spelled it out a bit more in the email. What he intended by this was really a paraphrase of the answer to the first question in the Westminster Shorter Catechism. There, it says that our 'chief end is to glorify God, and to enjoy Him forever'. I thought a reasonable subtitle was something like, 'How we Should Respond to the God who Has Rescued us'. After all, is that not the heart of worship, responding to the God who has rescued us? This is what I want to focus on here.

But what would be good place to go to think about this? Well, I thought to myself, I teach the Old Testament, so it needs to be the Old Testament. The more I reflected and prayed, the more suitable, I thought, was Deuteronomy 6:4–5: 'Hear, O Israel: The LORD our God, the LORD is one. You shall love the LORD your God with all your heart and with all your soul and with all your might.' After all, Jesus speaks of verse 5 as one of two verses on which the entire Old Testament hangs (Matt. 22:36–40). What is more, there are many parallels between the situation in Deuteronomy and our own. Let me set the scene, and you will see.

The scene, I am sure, is familiar. The people of Israel were gathered in the plains of Moab, on tiptoe, looking across the river Jordan. In front of them, over the Jordan, lay the Promised Land. Behind them lay a chequered past. The good parts were from God; the bad, from his people. Behind them lay God's promises made to Abraham: promises that they would be a great nation; promises of a land; promises of blessing (Gen. 12:1–3 etc.). Behind them lay God rescuing them from slavery in Egypt. Behind them lay their meeting with God at Mount Sinai. There, God had made a covenant with them – an agreement – and had given them laws which would shape who they were as his people. Behind them lay God's sustaining of them in the desert.

But also behind them lay a catalogue of failures. Almost all the people had grumbled and rebelled against God. They had wished they were back in Egypt, so God had punished them. The wicked first generation that God had rescued from Egypt had died out in the wilderness and would never enter the land.

Now, though, a new generation had grown up. Here, on the edge of the Promised Land, Moses addressed this second generation. Here, in the second part of his second sermon, Moses prepared the people for life in the land. His subject: 'How you should respond to the God who has rescued us', or 'How you should live in the land'.

This echoes back to Adam and Eve living in the Garden of Eden, under God's rule. They had received his commands, and were in a place of life if only they would obey. But they refused. In Deuteronomy, the same picture is held out again, a picture of living in a land reminiscent of Eden, under God's rule. The way of obedience is the way to life for a people rescued from slavery (see Deut. 30:15).

And are we not in a similar situation? In the New Testament, God's kingdom is all about living under God's rule. Again, this is a place of life, with echoes back to Eden. The way of obedience, trusting and obeying Jesus' words, is the way to life.

It is wonderful how neatly the Bible fits together!

But then I thought a bit further, because it is not that straightforward. For one thing, these verses are much misunderstood; for another, Israel is a nation, but we are the church; for another, when Moses was talking, the Word had not yet become flesh – Jesus of Nazareth had not yet walked on to the stage of history; and finally, what about the bits in Deuteronomy about killing the Canaanites?

Let's look more closely, then, at what Deuteronomy says to us as Christians. There are two truths from Deuteronomy about responding to the God who has rescued us.

Acclaim God alone: Deuteronomy 6:4

'Hear, O Israel, The LORD our God, the LORD is one!'

Although this phrase hardly puts in an appearance in the rest of the Old Testament, it is an amazingly significant phrase. It is known as the Shema, from the Hebrew for the first word, *Hear*. In the afterlife of the Old Testament, you can see how important it is from the fact that in some of the Dead Sea Scrolls found at

Qumran, it is placed next to the Ten Commandments. It remained critical throughout history in Jewish tradition, and even today orthodox Jews recite the phrase twice daily, when they wake up in the morning and again at night.

Notice the key parts of this. First, in the phrase 'the LORD our God', the word LORD is written in capitals. It is not a title, but God's name, Yahweh. It was in and through the great event of the exodus and the giving of the Law that God revealed himself to his people. His name, Yahweh, gained shape and definition from these events: he is Yahweh, the God who keeps his promises and rescues his people. So this is a name that they know and should hold dear, a name that speaks of the exodus, a name that speaks of God's faithfulness to his promises, a name that speaks of his rescue, of his giving of the Law. In short, it is a name full of meaning to them. 'Hear, O Israel, Yahweh – the God who rescues, the God who is faithful to his promises – Yahweh our God, Yahweh is One.'

But what does it mean to say that 'Yahweh is one'? There are lots of debates about how to translate it and what it means. In the NRSV, for instance, it is translated, 'Hear, O Israel: The LORD is our God, the LORD alone.' In my judgment, it is often misunderstood.

Some say it is to do with God's *essence*: that he is one God, not three or more, but that is not the point here at all. That is to read in later debates. Some say it is to do with God's *character:* that he is not fickle or changeable, but one in his actions. Yahweh is dependable, unlike other gods. That is of course true, but again, not the point here. Some say it is linked with the *agenda of Deuteronomy*, to insist on worship in one place, Jerusalem – something that was part of Josiah's reforms. Certainly, Josiah's reforms are closely linked with Deuteronomy (see, for instance, 2 Kgs 23:25), but this can hardly be right. None of the reforms in Deuteronomy or Kings pick up on 'one' as a slogan; and why should God being 'one' mean only one place of worship is appropriate? Some say the phrase is to do with *monotheism;* that there is in existence only one God. Again, this is of course true, and, in my judgment, Deuteronomy teaches that (4:35), as does the rest of Bible. But that is not the point here.

We need to do some detective work. The first clue comes from the context, from what follows verse 4. The right response to this call in verse 5 says, *Love*. In other words, the context is all about a relationship.

The second clue comes from the best parallel where *one* is used to describe someone in a way that mirrors this relational context. This comes in Song of Songs 6:8–9. Solomon speaks of his lover:

> There are sixty queens and eighty concubines,
>> and virgins without number.
> My dove, my perfect one, is *the only one* [literally, 'one'],
>> *the only one* of her mother [literally, 'one'],
>> pure to her who bore her.
> The young women saw her and called her blessed;
>> the queens and concubines also, and they praised her.

Here the dove, the young woman is *one* to her lover and her mother. This is not because there are no others in existence. She is not the only woman in the world! Almost certainly, she is not the only daughter. But there is something about the relationship – she matters in a way that others do not. They recognize her as unique because of who they are and who she is.

It is a bit like gazing lovingly into your boyfriend's or girlfriend's eyes, or into your husband's or wife's, and saying, 'You're the one for me!' To say 'Yahweh is one' is to say he is unique because of the nature of the relationship.

That we are on the right lines here comes from the third clue, which is the only time in the rest of the Old Testament that the Shema is clearly picked up. Zechariah 14:9 looks into the future, and declares, 'And the LORD will be king over all the earth. On that day the LORD will be one and his name one.'

This is clearly not about God's essence changing, so that he will be 'one' *then* while he is 'many' *now*; nor is it about God's character changing, so that he will be faithful and consistent *then*, while he is not *now*; nor is it even about how many gods there are in the world. It is not saying there will only be one God *then*, although there are many *now*.

Rather, it is to do with everyone acclaiming God as the king *then* although they do not *now*. He 'will be one'. All will acknowledge him as king, their king. They will not acclaim anyone else.

You can also see we are on the right lines from Deuteronomy

6:14–15, which comes soon after the Shema: 'You shall not go after other gods, the gods of the peoples who are around you, for the LORD your God in your midst is a jealous God, lest the anger of the LORD your God be kindled against you . . .'

Can you see what verse 4 is about, then? Acclaim God alone. Worship God alone. There is no place for other gods, no place for idols, no place for rivals. A unique relationship means an exclusive one. You can hardly say 'You are the one for me' to your husband or wife, and then have an affair with a colleague at work. You can hardly say 'You are the one for me' to your boyfriend or girlfriend and then go on a date with someone else. If you are going to respond to the rescuing God, acclaim him alone.

But, you might be thinking, 'Couldn't I hear this in a synagogue? Where does Jesus fit into this? What about the Spirit?' This is surely the right question to be asking. After all, we have the whole Bible, not just the Old Testament.

In the New Testament, it is Paul who shows us where Jesus fits in, in 1 Corinthians 8:1–6. Paul is writing a letter to the church in Corinth. The context is all about food and idols:

> Now concerning food offered to idols: we know that 'all of us possess knowledge'. This 'knowledge' puffs up, but love builds up. If anyone imagines that he knows something, he does not yet know as he ought to know. But if anyone loves God, he is known by God.

In the New Testament, there is much more about God's love for us than our love for God, but here, talk of our love for God gives an echo of Deuteronomy 6:5. Paul continues:

> Therefore, as to the eating of food offered to idols, we know that 'an idol has no real existence', and that 'there is no God but *one*.'

If you look at the final word of that sentence, does it remind you of anything?

> For although there may be so-called gods in heaven or on earth – as indeed there are many 'gods' and many 'lords' – yet *for us* there is *one God, the Father*, from whom are all things and for whom we exist, and *one*

Lord, Jesus Christ, through whom are all things and through whom we
exist.

I have already pointed out two links between this passage and
Deuteronomy. But I want you to notice particularly verses 5–6.
Even if there were other gods (which, says Paul in v. 4, and says
Moses, there are not), yet, verse 6, *for us* (notice the relational word)
*there is but one God, the Father, from whom all things came and for whom we
live; and there is but one Lord, Jesus Christ.*
Can you see what Paul has done here? He has split up two key
words in the Shema, *God* and *Lord*. He uses *God* and speaks of the
Father, but when he uses *Lord*, he speaks of Jesus Christ. In other
words, he has put Jesus within a clear statement that Israel's God is
the one and only God, the Creator of the world.
If you went to the temple in Jerusalem in Paul's day, you would
have found orthodox Jews saying the Shema. Paul says that Jesus
of Nazareth, the man who walked this earth, who hung on a cruel
cross, belongs inside this prayer, not outside. It is not really that
Jesus is the same as God, but rather, if you are going to talk about
God, Jesus needs to be there. What you say about Yahweh in the
Old Testament, you can and now should say about Jesus Christ.
Later, this becomes the principle that what may be said of the
Father may also be said of the Son. Also, when you encounter
Jesus, you encounter the reality of God. The glory of God is to be
found in the face of Jesus Christ.
Over the next few hundred years, the whole doctrine of the
Trinity came to be unpacked from Scripture. For you as a
Christian to respond rightly to the one who has rescued you, it is
not just 'Hear, O Israel, Yahweh our God Yahweh is one,' but,
'Hear, O Church, the Holy Trinity our God, the Holy Trinity is
one' (or, perhaps better, so you can get the force, 'the Holy Trinity
alone').
I have taken you on a bit of a journey, but it is a vital journey,
for it takes us right to the heart of what it means to respond rightly
to God: 'Acclaim God the Holy Trinity alone.' There is no place
for idols, no place for rivals, no place for other gods. It is a unique
relationship, so it is an exclusive one.
But what other gods? It could be the gods of Hinduism or

other religions, but I guess it is fairly obvious that you are not likely to dabble there.

Another god might be the great one that Jesus identified – 'Mammon' – the love of money. A friend of mine has just gone back to teaching after ten years. She has been shocked at how materialistic the teenagers are – far more than even a few years ago. Few of us are immune. When we have this new kitchen/lawn-mower/house/better-paid job or whatever, then we shall be happy and feel secure!

Or this other god could be giving the last word, the final truth, to particular values:

- 'Be tolerant of everything except intolerance.' A friend of mine recently organized an evening on 'Morality and the media'. Some of you may be wondering if there is any connection at all! But, in all seriousness, the purpose of the evening was to examine what responsibility the media had for morality in society. There were four panelists. Two out of the four insisted on this slogan as the ultimate arbiter of what we should think and do. Interestingly, they did not have any clear approach for deciding what is intolerable except by majority opinion. That, of course, leaves open the tyrannizing of the minority.

- 'It doesn't matter what you believe as long as you're sincere.' As a prospective parent of a child at secondary school, I have recently been doing the rounds of schools listening to the head teachers explain their philosophy and give their reasons why I should choose their school. One head declared that he was keen for the pupils to 'respect other people's opinions'. It sounds sensible and worthy, but it is incoherent. How can a teacher 'respect' the opinions of a pupil who insists that $10 \times 11 = 121$? Tolerance of people, respecting other people, which is a virtue, has been replaced in our culture by respecting other people's *opinions*, which is a vice. We need to treat *people* with dignity, while being willing to debate vigorously over whether their *opinions* are good or true.

- 'Eat, drink and be merry, for tomorrow we die.' This is the slogan of the pleasure lover. It is the slogan of one who is always after life's limit experiences, whether it be through alcohol, drugs or holidays of a lifetime.

- 'Liberty, equality and fraternity.' This of course is written into the
  French constitution. It speaks of some very important values.
  But they are not *ultimate* values.

Those who hold these different values may insist, 'I am not religious.' But as ultimate values they are false religions: they are idols.

The false god could be the 'one God' of the Qur'an. Do not be
confused because people say, 'Christians and Muslims are similar
because they believe in one God,' or when you hear the phrase
'The great monotheistic religions'. Do not be misled here. The
god of the Qur'an is a very different god. Only one is Trinity. For a
Christian to speak about God is to speak about a God who is
Trinity. We are to acclaim God alone, God the Holy Trinity, Father,
Son and Spirit. No other gods.

And here is the second way to respond to the God who has
rescued us.

Love God alone: Deuteronomy 6:5

Because of our relationship with this God, and because he is God
alone . . . *so*, 'You shall love the LORD your God with all your heart
and with all your soul and with all your might.'

There is often some confusion here. Many see these three words
together here and think we are observing some kind of Hebrew
anthropology, where the three combine together to describe the
whole person. But that is not the point at all. *Heart* speaks of the
will or the mind or, rarely, the emotions. Here, it sums up 'inner
being': all that you are on the inside. And the word translated *soul*
does not mean some non-physical part of you inside you, a kind of
'ghost in the machine', but your life. Literally, it means 'breath' or
'neck'. In English, you can see a similar type of connection in the
phrase 'risk your neck', in the sense of 'risk your life'. The third
word, *might* or 'strength' does not mean something internal to you
– your muscles, your effort, your determination. Rather, it means
your resources or wealth: your possessions. Together, Moses calls
the people to love God with their mind, their emotions, their life
(even to the point of laying it down) and their resources.

But as with verse 4, it needs to be read in the wider context. Before we look at the more positive side of this for us, we cannot duck something that is here. Love for God alone in Deuteronomy gives rise not just to the fine ethic of concern for the poor and the stranger. It also gives rise to chapter 7 and the command to destroy the Canaanites. Does this mean that as Christians we are to destroy the infidel?

No. For the Israelites, it was a particular command at a particular time. We need to read it as Christians in the light of the whole Bible. The strategy is different for the church. The church is to live by the cross, not by the sword. Jesus rebuked James and John for wanting to call down fire from heaven on the Samaritans who had rejected him (Luke 9:54). Jesus rebuked Peter for picking up a sword to defend him when Judas and the chief priests come to arrest him. Judgment will come, but it is not the job of God's people to bring it. The other New Testament command alongside 'Love the Lord your God with all your heart' is to 'Love your neighbour as yourself'.

Additional note on the slaughter of the Canaanites

There was not time in the sermon to say any more on this difficult subject. There are a few other points that I would make with more space:

- *The wickedness of the Canaanites* – some of the Canaanite religious practices were revolting and immoral, with sacred prostitution and children thrown into the fire as sacrifices. To give you some idea of its awfulness, the place where they burned and sacrificed children to Molech, their God, became the name for Jewish hell – Gehenna. Sometimes a surgeon has to amputate a limb to stop the gangrene spreading. Drastic action sometimes is right. Here is a case in point. The gangrene was so awful, that it needed wiping out. The nations were wicked and under God's judgment. Deuteronomy makes this point clearly: 'it is because of the wickedness of these nations that the LORD is driving them out before you' (Deut. 9:4).
- *The frailty and place of Israel* – the purpose of Israel was in part to show nations what God is like. Israel's election in Deuteronomy

7 was not nationalistic, but ultimately to show salvation to nations (cf. Gen. 12:1–3; Exod. 19:5–6; Deut. 4:6–8). However, Israel was a brittle nation, which tended to rebel. God's whole purpose in choosing Israel was in jeopardy with compromise here – as the rest of the Old Testament shows.

- *The consistency of God's action* – when God sees recurring wickedness within his own people after they have entered the land, they face the same judgment and expulsion from the land that the Canaanites faced (Deut. 4:25–26).
- *Anticipated eschatology* – this activity of God coming in judgment against wickedness in such severe fashion is not a case of arrested ethical development, but of anticipated eschatology. Central in the hope for the future in Jesus' day was an impending judgment on those who defied God. God would act to punish all wickedness. Jesus himself makes it clear that there'll be a judgment on those who reject God. He says that his disciples are to say in towns that reject them, 'I tell you, it will be more bearable on that day for Sodom than for that town' (Luke 10:12).

But there are things we can say more positively about the call to *Love Yahweh alone*. Can you see how loving God is not something niggardly and grudging? Notice how the word 'all' comes again and again: 'with *all* your heart and with *all* your soul and with *all* your might'? Everything is to be at God's disposal, even your very life – yes, your car, your PC, your house, your money, your time.

Can you see how loving God is not something legalistic or merely external? Do not listen to the caricatures of Old Testament religion. At the heart of responding to God is loving him, on the inside. This is something profoundly emotional and internal.

Can you see how loving God is something for all the family? Deuteronomy 6:6–7 says, 'And these words that I command you today shall be on your heart. You shall teach them diligently to your children, and shall talk of them when you sit in your house, and when you walk by the way, and when you lie down, and when you rise.' You are to talk about acclaiming God alone and loving God alone in your family setting. If you are a parent, you are responsible for your child's spiritual development. It is not the Sunday school teacher or the youth worker – *you* are. If you are a youth worker or youth leader or Sunday school teacher or help on summer camps, the young person's spiritual welfare is not your responsibility. You are there to assist the parents.

Can you see how loving God is not something private? Look at verses 8–9. The words are to be between their eyes and on their doorposts. Everyone is to know who is your God, that you acclaim God the Holy Trinity alone; you love God the Holy Trinity alone.

Can you see how loving God is not something sentimental? While it involves emotions, it is shaped by the Scriptures. At the heart of it are the Scriptures: 'And these words that I command you today shall be on your heart' (Deut. 6:6). You only have to think of Jesus' words 'If you love me, you will keep my commandments' (John 14:15).

But for many of us, maybe the problem is not knowledge. We *know* this. Our problem is *doing* it. It is a problem of our will, or a problem of our action. So I wonder if I may go beyond outlining how we should respond, and ask, 'Will you respond this way? Will you acclaim God the Holy Trinity alone? Will you love him alone? Will you draw on the Spirit's resources today, so that you do just that?'

BIBLIOGRAPHY

Alexander, T. D. and Rosner, B. (eds.) (2000), *New Dictionary of Biblical Theology*, (Leicester: Inter-Varsity Press).

Ames, W. (1997), *The Marrow of Theology*, trans. of 3rd Latin edn 1629, J. D. Eusden, 1968 (Grand Rapids: Baker).

Baker, D. W. (ed.) (2001), *Looking into the Future: Evangelical Studies in Eschatology* (Grand Rapids: Baker).

Balz, H. and Schneider, G. (eds.) (1990), *Exegetical Dictionary of the New Testament*, vol. 1 (Edinburgh: T. & T. Clark).

Barrett, C. K. (1978), *The Gospel According to St John*, 2nd edn. (London: SPCK).

Bauckham, R. J. (1980), 'The Delay of the Parousia', *TynBul* 31:3–36.

Bauckham, R. J. (ed.) (1998), *The Gospels for All Christians: Rethinking the Gospel Audiences* (Grand Rapids: Eerdmans).

Bauckham, R. J. (2001), 'The Audience of the Fourth Gospel', in R.C. Fortna and T. Thatcher (eds.), *Jesus in Johannine Tradition* (London: Westminster John Knox), pp. 101–111.

Beale, G. K. (2004), *The Temple and the Church's Mission: A Biblical Theology of the Dwelling Place of God* (Leicester: Apollos).

Beasley-Murray, G. R. (1986), *Jesus and the Kingdom of God* (Grand Rapids: Eerdmans/Carlisle: Paternoster).

Beasley-Murray, G. R. (1987), *John* (2nd edn 1999) (Waco: Word).

Beasley-Murray, G. R (1991), *Gospel of Life: Theology in the Fourth Gospel* (Peabody: Hendrickson).

Berlin, I. (1997), 'Vico and the Ideal of the Enlightenment', in H. Hardy and R. Hausheer (eds.), *Against the Current: Essays in the History of Ideas* (London: Pimlico), pp. 25–78.

Berlin, I. (1998a), 'The Pursuit of the Ideal', in H. Hardy and R. Hausheer (eds.), *The Proper Study of Mankind* (London: Pimlico), pp. 1–16.

Berlin, I. (1998b), 'Two Concepts of Liberty', in H. Hardy and R. Hausheer (eds.), *The Proper Study of Mankind* (London: Pimlico), pp. 191–242.

Berlin, I. (1998c), 'The Originality of Machiavelli', in H. Hardy and R. Hausheer (eds.), *The Proper Study of Mankind* (London: Pimlico), pp. 269–325.

Black, D. A. (1998), *It's Still All Greek to Me: An Easy-to-Understand Guide to Intermediate Greek* (Grand Rapids: Baker).

Block, D. I. (2004), 'How Many Is God? An Investigation Into the Meaning of Deuteronomy 6:4–5', *JETS* 47: 193–212.

Blomberg, C. L. (1987), *The Historical Reliability of the Gospels* (Leicester: Inter-Varsity Press).

Blomberg, C. L. (1992), *Matthew*, NAC (Nashville: Broadman).

Blomberg, C. L. (2001a), 'The Historical Reliability of John: Rushing in where Angels Fear to Tread?' in R. C. Fortna and T. Thatcher (eds.), *Jesus in Johannine Tradition* (London: Westminster John Knox), pp. 71–82.

Blomberg, C. L. (2001b), *The Historical Reliability of John's Gospel* (Leicester: Apollos).

Bock, D. L. (1994), *Luke: The IVP New Testament Commentary Series* (Downers Grove: InterVarsity Press).

Bock, D. L. (2001), 'The Kingdom of God in NT Theology: The Battle, the Christ, the Spirit-Bearer, and Returning Son of Man', in D. W Baker. (ed.), *Looking into the Future: Evangelical Studies in Eschatology* (Grand Rapids: Baker), pp. 28–60.

Bolt, P. (2004), *The Cross from a Distance: Atonement in Mark's Gospel* (Leicester: Apollos).

Borchert, G. L. (1996), *John 1–11* (Nashville: Broadman & Holman).

Brown, R. (1970), *The Gospel According to St John XIII–XXI* (New York: Doubleday).

Brown, R. (1982), *The Epistles of John* (New York: Doubleday).

Bruce, F. F. (1981), *Paul, Apostle of the Free Spirit* (Carlisle: Paternoster).

Bultmann, R. (1952), *Theology of the New Testament*, vol. 1 (ET, London: SCM, 1952).

Bultmann, R. (1971), *The Gospel of John*, trans. G. Beasley-Murray (Oxford: Blackwell).

Burge, G. (1987), *The Anointed Community: The Holy Spirit in the Johannine Tradition* (Grand Rapids: Eerdmans).

Burge, G. (2000), *John: NIVAC* (Grand Rapids: Zondervan).

Caird, G. B. (1994), *New Testament Theology* (Oxford: Clarendon).

Calvin, J. (1959), *The Gospel According to St John*, vol. 1 (Grand Rapids: Eerdmans).

Campbell, D. A. (2005), *The Quest for Paul's Gospel: A Suggested Strategy*, JSNTSup 274 (London: Continuum).

Caragounis, C. C. (1989), 'Kingdom of God, Son of Man and Jesus' Self-Understanding', *TynBul* 40:3–23, 223–238.

Caragounis, C. C. (1992a), 'The Kingdom of God in John and the Synoptics', in A. Denaux (ed.), *John and the Synoptics* (Leuven: Leuven University Press), pp. 473–480.

Caragounis, C. C. (1992b), 'Kingdom of God/Heaven', in J. B. Green, S. McKnight and I. H. Marshall (eds.), *The Dictionary of Jesus and the Gospels* (Downers Grove: InterVarsity Press), pp. 417–430.

Caragounis, C. C. (2001), 'The Kingdom of God: Common and Distinct Elements between John and the Synoptics', in R. C. Fortna and T. Thatcher (eds.), *Jesus in Johannine Tradition* (London: Westminster John Knox) pp. 125–134.

Caragounis, C. C. (2004), 'Does the Aorist Indicative Support Realized Eschatology?', in *The Development of Greek and the New Testament: Morphology, Syntax, Phonology, and Textual Transmission* (Tübingen: Mohr-Siebeck), pp. 261–278.

Carson, D. A. (1981), *Divine Sovereignty and Human Responsibility: Biblical Perspectives in Tension* (London: Marshall, Morgan & Scott).

Carson, D. A. (1982), 'Understanding Misunderstandings in the Fourth Gospel', *TynBul* 33:59–91.

Carson, D. A. (1991), *The Gospel According to John* (Leicester: Apollos).

Chesterton, G. K. (1909), *Orthodoxy* (London: Bodley Head).

Collins, J. J. (1993), *Daniel* (Minneapolis: Fortress).

Conquest, R. (1968), *The Great Terror* (London: Macmillan).

Conzelmann, H. (1960), *The Theology of St Luke*, trans. G. Buswell (New York: Harper & Row).

Dalman, G. (1909), *The Words of Jesus* (Edinburgh: T. & T. Clark).

Dillistone, F. W. (1977), *C. H. Dodd: Interpreter of the New Testament* (London: Hodder & Stoughton).

Dodd, C. H. (1936), *The Apostolic Preaching and its Developments* (London: Hodder & Stoughton, repr. Grand Rapids: Baker, 1980).

Dodd, C. H. (1953), *The Interpretation of the Fourth Gospel* (Cambridge: CUP).

Dunn, J. D. G. (1970a), 'Spirit and Kingdom', *ExpT* 82:36–40.

Dunn, J. D. G. (1970b), *Baptism in the Holy Spirit* (London: SCM).

Dunn, J. D. G. (1971), 'John VI A Eucharistic Discourse?', *NTS* 17:328–338.

Dunn, J. D. G. (1977), *Unity and Diversity in the New Testament: An Inquiry into the Character of Earliest Christianity* (London: SCM).

Dunn, J. D. G. (1985), *The Evidence for Jesus* (London: SCM).

France, R. T. (1990), *Divine Government* (London: SPCK).

Fuller, R. H. (1967), 'The Mission and Achievement of Jesus', *SBT* 12 (London: SCM).

Gathercole, S. J. (2003), 'The Cross and Substitutionary Atonement', *SBET* 21.2:152–165.

Gathercole, S. J. (2004a), 'Justified by Faith, Justified by his Blood: The Evidence of Rom. 3.21–4.25', in D. A. Carson, P. T. O'Brien and M. A. Seifrid (eds.), *Justification and Variegated Nomism*. Vol. 2: *The Paradoxes of Paul*, WUNT (Tübingen: Mohr), pp. 147–184.

Gathercole, S. J. (2004b), 'The Son of Man in Mark's Gospel', *ExpT* 115: 366–372.

Gathercole, S. J. (2005), 'The Pauline and Petrine *Sola Fide*', in M. Bachmann (ed.), *Lutherische oder Neue Paulusperspektive?* WUNT (Tübingen: Mohr), pp. 309–327.

Giles, K. (1981), 'Present–Future Eschatology in the Book of Acts (1)', *RTR* 40.3 (Sept.–Dec.), pp. 65–71.

Giles, K. (1982), 'Present–Future Eschatology in the Book of Acts (2)', *RTR* 41.1 (Jan.–Apr.), pp. 11–18.

Goodacre, M. (2001), *The Synoptic Problem: A Way through the Maze*, Biblical Seminar 80 (London: Continuum).

Goppelt, L. (1982), *Theology of the New Testament*, vol. 1 (Grand Rapids: Eerdmans).

Green, C. (2005), *The Word of His Grace* (Leicester: Inter-Varsity Press).

Green, J. B. (1997), *The Gospel of Luke*, NICNT (Grand Rapids: Eerdmans).

Green, J. B. (1998), '"Salvation to the End of the Earth" (Acts 13:47): God as Saviour in the Acts of the Apostles', in I. H. Marshall and D. G. Peterson (eds.), *Witness to the Gospel: The Theology of Acts* (Grand Rapids: Eerdmans), pp. 83–106.

Green, J. B., McKnight, S. and Marshall, I. H. (eds.) (1992), *The Dictionary of Jesus and the Gospels* (Downers Grove: InterVarsity Press).

Gundry, R. H. (1993), *Mark: A Commentary on His Apology for the Cross* (Grand Rapids: Eerdmans).

Guthrie, D. (1981), *New Testament Theology* (Leicester: Inter-Varsity Press).

Hays, J. D. (2003), *From Every Race and Nation: A Biblical Theology of Race* (Leicester: Apollos/Downers Grove, InterVarsity Press).

Hengel, M. (1984), *Die Evangelienüberschriften* (Heidelberg: Carl Winter).

Hengel, M. and Schwemer, A.-M. (1997), *Paul between Damascus and Antioch: The Unknown Years* (London: SCM).

Henry, C. F. H. (1992), 'Reflections on the Kingdom of God', *JETS* 35.1:39–50.

Hooker, M. D. (1991), *The Gospel According to St Mark* (London: Black).

Johnson, D. H. (1992), 'Life', in J. B. Green, S. McKnight and I. H. Marshall (eds.), *The Dictionary of Jesus and the Gospels* (Downers Grove: InterVarsity Press), pp. 469–471.

Jonge, M. de (1992), 'The Radical Eschatology of the Fourth Gospel and the Eschatology of the Synoptics', in Denaux A. (ed.), *John and the Synoptics* (Leuven: Leuven University Press), pp. 481–487.

Käsemann, E. (1968), *The Testament of Jesus: A Study of the Gospel of John According to John 17* (Philadelphia: Fortress).

Keener, C. S. (1999), *A Commentary on the Gospel of Matthew*, 2 vols. (Grand Rapids: Eerdmans).

Keener, C. S. (2003), *The Gospel of John* (Peabody: Hendrickson).

Kim, S. (1983), *The Son of Man as the Son of God* (Grand Rapids: Eerdmans).

Köstenberger, A. J. (2004), *John* (Grand Rapids: Baker).

Kruse, C. (2003), *The Gospel According to John* (Leicester: Inter-Varsity Press).

Kysar, R. (1975), *The Fourth Evangelist and His Gospel* (Minneapolis: Augsburg).

Ladd, G. E. (1974), *The Presence of the Future* (Grand Rapids: Eerdmans).

Ladd, G. E. (1975), *A Theology of the New Testament* (Cambridge: Lutterworth).

Lane, W. L. (1974), *The Gospel According to Mark* (London: Marshall, Morgan & Scott).

Leithart, P. J. (2000), *A House for My Name: A Survey of the Old Testament* (Moscow: Canon).

Lindars, B. (1980–1), 'John and the Synoptic Gospels: A Test Case', *NTS* 27:287–294.

Louw, J. P. and Nida, E. A. (1992), *Lexical Semantics of the Greek New Testament: A Supplement to the Greek–English Lexicon of the New Testament Based on Semantic Domains* (Atlanta: Society of Biblical Literature).

Lowe, J. (1941), 'An Examination of Attempts to Detect Development in St Paul's Theology', *JTS* 42:129–142.

Lucas, E. C. (2002), *Daniel* (Leicester: Apollos).

Maccoby, H. (1986), *The Mythmaker: Paul and the Invention of Christianity* (London: HarperCollins).

Machiavelli, N. (1970), *The Discourses* (Harmondsworth: Penguin).

Marcus, J. (1992), *The Way of the Lord: Christological Exegesis of the Old Testament in the Gospel of Mark* (Louisville: Westminster John Knox).

Marcus, J. (2000), 'Mark: Interpreter of Paul', *NTS* 46:473–487.

Marshall, I. H. (ed.) (1990), *Jesus the Saviour: Studies in New Testament Theology* (London: SPCK).

Marshall, I. H. (1992), 'Son of Man', in J.B. Green, S. McKnight and I. H. Marshall (eds.), *The Dictionary of Jesus and the Gospels* (Downers Grove: InterVarsity Press), pp. 775–781.

Marshall, I. H. and Peterson, D. G. (eds.) (1998), *Witness to the Gospel: The Theology of Acts* (Grand Rapids: Eerdmans).

Moberly, R. W. L. (1990), 'Yahweh Is One: The Translation of the Shema', in J. A. Emerton (ed.), *Studies in the Pentateuch*, VTSup 41 (Leiden: Brill), pp. 209–215.

Moberly, R. W. L. (1999), Toward an Interpretation of the Shema', in C. R. Seitz and K. Greene-McCreight (eds.), *Theological Exegesis: Essays in Honor of Brevard A. Childs* (Grand Rapids: Eerdmans), pp. 124–144.

Moloney, F. J. (1978), *The Johannine Son of Man* (Rome: LAS).

Moloney, F. J. (1998), *The Gospel of John* (Collegeville: Liturgical).

Moo, D. J. (1997), *The Epistle to the Romans*, NICNT (Grand Rapids: Eerdmans).

Morris, L. (1989), *Jesus Is the Christ: Studies in the Theology of John* (Leicester: Inter-Varsity Press).

Morris, L. (1995), *The Gospel According to John* (Grand Rapids: Eerdmans).

Mounce, W. D. (2000), *The Pastoral Epistles,* WBC 46 (Nashville: Thomas Nelson).

Nolland, J. (1998), 'Salvation-History and Eschatology', in I. H. Marshall and D. G. Peterson (eds.), *Witness to the Gospel: The Theology of Acts* (Grand Rapids: Eerdmans), pp. 63–81.

O'Toole, R. F. (1979), 'Luke's Understanding of Jesus' Resurrection–Ascension–Exaltation', *BTB* 9:106–114.

O'Toole, R. F. (1981), 'Activity of the Risen Jesus in Acts', *Biblica* 62:471–498.

Parsons, M. C. (1987), *The Departure of Jesus in Luke–Acts: The Ascension Narratives in Context*, JSNTSup 21 (Sheffield: JSOT).

Perriman, A. C. (1989), 'Paul and the Parousia: 1 Cor. 15:50–57 and 2 Cor. 5:1–5', *NTS* 5:512–521.

Peterson, D. G. (ed.) (2003), *The Word Became Flesh: Evangelicals and the Incarnation* (Carlisle: Paternoster).

Peterson, D. G. (2004), 'Atonement Theology in Luke–Acts: Some Methodological Reflections', in P. J. Williams, A. D Clarke., P. M. Head and D. Instone-Brewer (eds.), *The New Testament in its First Century Setting: Essays on Context and Background, in Honour of B. W. Winter* (Grand Rapids: Eerdmans), pp. 56–71.

Porter, S. E. (1994), *Idioms of the Greek New Testament*, 2nd edn (Sheffield: Sheffield Academic Press).

Pryor, J. W. (1991), 'John 3:3, 5. A Study in the Relationship of John's Gospel to the Synoptic Tradition', *JSNT* 41:71–95.

Ridderbos, H. (1997), *The Gospel According to John* (Grand Rapids: Eerdmans).

Saunders, J. N. and Mastin, B. A. (1968), *A Commentary on the Gospel According to St John* (London: A. & C. Black).

Schaeffer, F. (1968), *The God Who Is There* (London: Hodder & Stoughton).

Schnackenburg, R. (1980), *John*, 3 vols. (London: Burns & Oates).

Scholtissek, K. (2004), 'The Johannine Gospel in Recent Research', in S. McKnight and G. R. Osborne (eds.), *The Face of New Testament Studies* (Leicester: Apollos), pp. 444–472.

Schweitzer, A. (1945), *The Quest of the Historical Jesus: A Critical Study of its Progress from Reimarus to Wrede* (London: A. & C. Black).

Schweitzer, A. (2000), *The Quest of the Historical Jesus: First Complete Edition* (London: SCM).

Smalley, S. (1964), 'The Delay of the Parousia', *JBL* 83:41–54.

Smalley, S. (1998), *John: Evangelist and Interpreter*, 2nd edn (Carlisle: Paternoster).

Stonehouse, N. B. (1944), *The Witness of Matthew and Mark to Christ* (London: Tyndale).

Sylva, D. D. (ed.) (1990), *Reimaging the Death of the Lukan Jesus* (Frankfurt: Anton Hain).

Tannehill, R. (1990), *The Narrative Unity of Luke-Acts* (Minneapolis: Fortress Augsburg).

Thiselton, A. C. (2000), *The First Epistle to the Corinthians*, NIGTC (Grand Rapids: Eerdmans).

Thompson, M. M. (1992), 'John, Gospel of', in J. B. Green, S. McKnight and I. H. Marshall (eds.), *The Dictionary of Jesus and the Gospels* (Downers Grove: InterVarsity Press), pp. 368–383.

Thornton, C.-J. (1991), *Der Zeuge des Zeugen: Lukas als Historiker der Paulusreisen*, (WUNT; Tübingen: Mohr).

Tyson, J. B. (1986), *The Death of Jesus in Luke–Acts* (Columbia: University of South Carolina Press).

Wallace, D. B. (1996), *Greek Grammar Beyond the Basics: An Exegetical Syntax of the New Testament* (Grand Rapids: Zondervan).

Wenham, D. (1997), *The Book of Signs – John's Gospel: Good News for Today* (Leicester: Religious and Theological Students Fellowship).

Wenham, J. (1965), *The Elements of New Testament Greek*, 1st edn (Cambridge: CUP).

Williams, B. (1979), 'Conflicts of Values', in A. Ryan (ed.), *The Idea of Freedom: Essays in Honour of Isaiah Berlin* (Oxford: OUP), pp. 221–232.

Williams, P. J., Clarke, A. D., Head, P. M. and Instone-Brewer, D. (eds.) (2004), *The New Testament in its First Century Setting: Essays on Context and Background, in Honour of B. W. Winter* (Grand Rapids: Eerdmans).

Willis, W. (ed.) (1987), *The Kingdom of God in 20th-Century Interpretation* (Peabody: Hendrickson).

Witherington, B. III (1992), *Jesus, Paul and the End of the World* (Exeter: Paternoster).

Witherington, B. III (1995), *John's Wisdom: A Commentary on the Fourth Gospel* (Cambridge: Lutterworth).

Witherington, B. III (1997), 'Transcending Imminence: The Gordian Knot of Pauline Eschatology', in K. Brower and M. W Elliott. (ed.), *'The Reader Must Understand': Eschatology in Bible and Theology* (Leicester: Apollos), pp. 171–186.

Wright, N. T. (1991), 'Monotheism, Christology and Ethics: 1 Corinthians 8', in *The Climax of the Covenant: Christ and the Law in Pauline Theology* (Edinburgh: T. & T. Clark), pp. 120–136.

Wright, N. T. (1997), *What St Paul Really Said: Was Paul of Tarsus the Real Founder of Christianity?* (Oxford: Lion).

Wright, N. T. (2003), *The Resurrection of the Son of God* (London: SPCK).